Letters FROM HELL

Letters FROM

H.E.L.L.

REVEALING THE RESTORATION POWER OF ALMIGHTY
GOD TO THOSE ENGAGED IN THE SAVAGE
BRUTALITY OF DRUG & ALCOHOL ADDICTION,
SEXUAL PERVERSION AND POOR CHOICES

RICHARD W. HEADRICK

HELLFIGHTER PUBLICATIONS

ISBN 978-0-9823523-7-3
Library of Congress Control Number: 2013916683

Cover design and layout by SeedStudios.com

Acknowledgements

We would like to thank Lynn Lyon, Vaughn Blackwell, Danny Stringer and Jerry Yandell for unselfishly participating in this project by not only corresponding with those who wrote these and other letters from hell, but also by packing and shipping, from our warehouse, thousands of Bibles, tracts and t-shirts.

We are especially thankful to Robert Smith who, having been an addict himself, knows firsthand what these men and ladies are going through. Some of his responses have been included in this book. You will find godly wisdom in each of them.

"A League of Extraordinary
Ladies & Gentlemen
Who Are On Fire For Jesus!"

Table of Contents

Proverbs 4:14-15, 19

Enter not into the path of the wicked, and go not in the way of evil men. Avoid it, pass not by it, turn from it, and pass away.

The way of the wicked is as darkness; they know not at what they stumble.

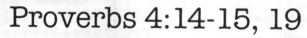

Proverbs 4:18

But the path of the just is as the shining light, that shineth more and more unto the perfect day.

Preface

In the late 1990s, my wife and I embarked upon a seventeen-year journey that would forever change our lives. This journey didn't take us to five star hotels, fine dining restaurants and top tourist attractions in exotic places to experience the finer things in life and learn about culture, architecture, history and art. To the contrary, we embarked upon a journey into a world of depravity and loneliness to experience the plight of the homeless and those who are prisoners of addictions by spending our weekends dressed as homeless vagrants, sleeping outside, with no money or food.

To accomplish our mission of finding out exactly how someone in this station of life is treated, we did not target the skid rows and ghetto areas of our country, even though we did spend time in these areas of hopelessness. We didn't wander the downtown areas of big cities or the neighborhoods of small villages. No! We targeted the Christian community, better known as America's churches.

Our story of this eye-opening adventure, which we call "The Bum Thing," can be found in the best selling book America's Churches through the Eyes of a Bum. Throughout those seventeen years, we were treated by some as if we were royalty, but most of the time we were treated as if we were the scourge of the earth—enemies of society. We found out what it was like to feel despised and unwanted. In other words, we were treated like most folks treat Jesus.

We did discover that there are a lot of good people in America's churches. We also found that there are a lot of good people who never darken the door of America's churches. Sadly however, neither group knows how to treat people who look, smell, dress and act differently than they do.

Danny Stringer, a dear friend of ours, came to work with us as our companies' chief pilot. Gina and I don't fly as much as we used to, so "Sky King," as Danny is called, has quite a bit of spare time. During his spare time, Sky King corresponds with prison inmates and men from various rescue missions on behalf of a ministry we have called Hellfighters. Not only does he communicate words of encouragement to them, but he also sends them a Hellfighter New Testament or a big print Bible, along with a Satan Sucks t-shirt. Over the years, this process of communication has allowed us to accumulate thousands of hand-written letters from men and women who have found themselves prisoners of addiction, all because of bad choices.

As we began to learn more and more about this world of pain and desperation through doing "The Bum Thing" and corresponding with inmates and addicts, we felt led to do something about their plight.

In 2007, God impressed me and Gina to build a rescue mission in Sturgis, SD. As strange as it may seem, that mission is only open two weeks out of the year. Why? Because the annual Black Hills Motorcycle Rally, which began as a week-long event, now stretches out to two weeks, and 500,000 bikers show up every year to take in the events.

However, many of the revelers can't handle their women, whiskey or drugs. We're there for them.

In 2008, we began work on our flagship rescue mission, Mission at the Cross, in our hometown of Laurel, MS which is open 24/7/365 and offers free room, board and a 6+ month Christ-centered recovery program for those who truly desire to get their lives back. Today, Mission at the Cross Facilities can be found in Laurel, MS; Sturgis, SD; Richmond, IN; Chipley, FL; Gastonia, NC; Batesville, AR and Gramelow, Germany. Lord willing, there will be 100 Mission at the Cross Facilities operating one day. The need is great.

What we have seen during our seventeen years of pretending to be homeless, through our correspondence with thousands of prison inmates and recovery center clients, as well as our "hands on" experiences at our local Mission at the Cross Facility, has motivated us to share with you a glimpse into life as they know it-the horror of drugs, the hellish effects of alcohol, the heart-breaking ravages of financial ruin, the pain of broken marriages, the grief of desperate spouses and the hate of rebellious children.

This book contains photo copies of the actual handwritten letters from those who have allowed us to share their stories. Some have been resized to fit the page for easier reading. You will notice that names, dates and sometimes entire sentences have been scratched out to protect the identity of the person who wrote each letter. You will notice many misspelled words, bad grammar and wrong tenses in many of the letters, which sometimes make them difficult to understand. This further emphasizes the affect drugs and alcohol have on a person, regardless of their age or station in life.

In many of these letters, you will find the names of the actual recovery centers, where the writer of each of these letters resided for a period of time, are blocked out and replaced with Mission, Rehab Center, Rehab Facility, Recovery Center, etc. We opted to do this so that no one's identity could be compromised by someone putting 2 + 2 together. We have done our best to conceal the writer's identity. However, there are some recovery facilities' names left in the text, but the names of those writers are generic or they have also been changed. Otherwise, what you are about to read are their uncensored letters to us. As you absorb these letters into the recesses of your mind, know that they are but a sampling of the millions of letters that have already been written, by individuals who let Satan ruin their lives, and the tens of thousands of similar letters being written as you read this book.

The purpose of sharing these letters, some of which contain very personal and private details of a person's life, is not to exploit their circumstances or their poor judgment. Rather, it is in hopes that, by reading about others' mistakes and the resulting consequences, you or a loved one may avoid similar torment and ruin by being warned what WILL happen should you ever decide to experiment with

Satan's enticing temptations.

If you have a story you think would help a kid, a mama, a daddy, a husband or a wife stay clear of what drugs, alcohol and the negligence of self-discipline will do to the unprepared, then send it to us and we'll consider putting it in the second edition of Letters from Hell.

Oh, by the way, Satan has a word for you: "I have come to steal everything that's dear to you; I have come to kill every dream you dream, and last, but not least, I have come to destroy everything that's good and wholesome in your life" (John 10:10, paraphrased).

Now, this writer has a word for you... DON'T LET HIM!

Be alert and on guard! Because your arch enemy, the devil, roams to and fro across the land searching for someone, just like you, to destroy (1 Peter 5:8, paraphrased).

All Addicts Are Liars

Thank you so much for the pamphlet. It was inspirational. I'm here at the mission ▓▓▓▓ because the abuse of alcohol has turned me into someone I don't like. And I'm sure God's not pleased.

I'm so tired of being myself. Of messing up things the way I do. It's a tiredness not lost in sleep, and only worse in waking. I can't help thinking how great it would be to start anew. A really clean slate. It's the only thing left that excites me.

It doesn't matter what you are addicted to. Be it alcohol, drugs, sex, food, gambling, etc. If you are a slave to anything, you are in trouble; you are an addict, period. And all addicts are liars - masters of deception. You know why that is? Because once we look in the mirror and see what's really there, we have only two choices. Go straight to hell, or go through hell to get straight.

Sincerely,

RH's Note: I know the writer of this letter personally. He is the great grandson of one of the most prestigious advertising firms in North America. It just goes to show that Satan is no respecter of persons, so whether you live under a bridge or in a high rise condo, Satan wants to destroy you.

A Voice Said, "Kill Him"

Mr. Hellfighter;

KILL...

Noooooooooooooooooo!!!!!!

How are you doing my name is ████████
I'am 22 years old and from ██████, Louisiana.
Around this time last year I was kinda hiding
out in Texas. I think it was on a Friday night
I was at my Aunts house and we were boiling
crawfish. I must have taken about ten Zantex that day
along with a case of beer. As time passed by, me and
my aunt start arguing and cussing at each other. Now
she had her boyfriend their also, I had never met him
before at all. Anyway, he stepped in the picture and tells
me to watch my mouth or something like that. And
man, did I flip out. I didn't say anything, but
something in my head said "Just kill this dude"! So,
quietly I walked two houses down to my moms. Went
to my old bedroom closet. Grabbed my 12-guage shotgun,
one shotgun shell, and headed back. By this time my
moms screaming at me because they seen how wasted
I was. Plus I think they had a idea of what I was
about to do. It was dark outside, so my aunt and
her boyfriend really couldn't see me coming. I got
about 20 yards from them, they were sitting at
a table outside. I pointed the gun, pulled the hammer
back, and right as I squeezed the trigger, something
changed my mind and I pointed it in the air.
So, about that time my daughters mother drove by

unexpectedly and I jumped in with her. Thats about
as good as I remember that night because I was really
wasted and Zanex doesn't help you remember to good.
But I know I heard a voice tell me to kill him
and to this day I still ~~quiver~~ quiver when I think
about that. Because that was the devil who whispered
to me. So, I left town the next morning not really
remembering to much of what I did. A couple days later
I called my aunt to tell her I was sorry. And
she broke down and said that there were two kids
outside sitting at the table with them. WOW!!
I was so drunk that I didn't even see kids.
        Then God stepped in and said!
Are you tired of living like this? Do you want
a better life? I can give you this. And about
2 months later Teen Challenge came into my life
And God has worked miraculous things im my life.
I have been restored with my family. I get to see
my daughter again. I have peace, no desire for drugs
any more. But a desire for ministry. I complete in
2½ months. And will be working for this ministry
for another year or untill I hear from God.
Oh yeah, Ed████████ referred me.
                                    Thank you

Waylen says Hi & thanks

4

RH's Note:
Every letter that we receive gets a response from one of our Hellfighter volunteers. Scattered throughout this book you will see a few of the responses written by Robert Smith. Space would not allow us to include all of the responses, but we hope they will be an encouragement to you.

BOOK 3. OF INNER COMFORT

Chapter 2

That Truth Speaks Quietly to the Heart

Disciple:

Speak, Lord, for your servant is listening. I am your servant; give me understanding that I may know your ways. Incline my heart to your words, and let your speech come upon me as dew upon the grass. In days gone by the children of Israel said to Moses, ''Speak to us and we shall listen; do not let the Lord speak to us, lest we die.'' This is not how I pray, Lord. No. With the great prophet Samuel, I humbly and earnestly beg: ''Speak, Lord, for your servant is listening.''

Do not let Moses or any other prophet speak to me. You speak to me, O Lord God, you who inspire and enlighten all the prophets, for you alone, without them, can perfectly instruct me, while they without you can do nothing. They indeed can utter words, but they cannot convey the spirit of those words. They say beautiful things, but with you silent, they do not set the heart on fire. They convey the letter, but you reveal the meaning. They pronounce the mysteries, but you unfold their secrets. They declare the commandments, but you help us to practice them. They point out the way, but you give us the strength to walk it. They work only from the outside, but you instruct and enlighten the heart. They water the surface, but you provide a rich harvest. They proclaim the words, but you give understanding to what we hear.

So, do not let Moses speak to me, but you, O Lord, my God, eternal Truth, you speak to me. If I hear your voice, I may not die dry and barren as I would if I were warned from without and not inflamed from within. If I hear your voice, may I not be condemned for hearing the word and not following it, for knowing it and not loving it, for believing it and not living it. Speak then, Lord, for your servant listens, for you have the words of eternal life. Speak to me to comfort my soul and to change my whole life; in turn, may it give you praise and glory and honor, forever and ever.

Dear ████,

Man, you've got alot of years ahead of you, (Lord willing), make good use of your time, Eph. 5:15-1 Col. 4:5. Learn, this takes time, to Listen to the Holy Spirit, Is. 30:2 He will guide you, Ps. 16:11, protect & give you strength, Is. 49:16, Phil. 4:13, Ps. 27:1, 84:11. He will never leave you, Heb. 13:5,6. Listen to Wise Counsel, Pro. 1:5, Ps. 33:11, 119:24. GOD loves you, Jn. 3:16, Rm. 5:8. Write to me sometime Love in Christ Robert G. Smith ➤ Rev. 21 Heaven ♥

Addicted to Everything

My life, just like everyone else's life, has been full of choices. The difference is that I made a lot of bad choices, and usually did so willingly. At this point in my life I don't know why I wanted to do some of the things I have done, especially the things that have prevented me from obtaining the life I want — and happiness. Maybe you can tell me why.

My name is ▆▆▆▆▆▆▆▆. Actually, it is Specialist ▆▆▆▆▆▆▆ ▆▆▆▆▆, a member of the Army National Gaurd. There — within the ranks of the Army, I'm a medic. Enough of a medic that my drug problem has been overlooked by my unit; which happens to be a ▆▆▆▆▆▆▆▆▆ company, for over six years.

I came from a pretty decent family. Parents divorced

at age four. Mom was a drug addict and never came around. My dad remarried when I was eight. My brothers were six and four. The step mom, as far as my feelings and thoughts are concerned, never cared for me or one of my brothers at all. But all of that is a different story, and I don't think that really matters.

I started smoking pot in junior high, and by high school had taken almost all of the prescription drugs available at the time. Sometime in Junior High I started drinking. I'm not too sure how that began, but I know I was stealing out of ~~their~~ my parents liquor cabinet and taking it to school ~~in~~ with my lunch.

By high school I was well down my trail to destruction. Drinking heavily, taking pills, and smoking pot, I still managed to make good grades and ~~maintain~~ excel at both football and baseball. Because of this, my parents either remained dumb to my issues, or simply overlooked them. I graduated high school with honors, and was offered a full scholarship to a junior college for academics. I was also spoken to by the coach from the ████ State University baseball team.

My choice came as a surprise to my family. Instead of going to college, I joined the Army National Guard. My family was more than willing to pay for my schooling, but I didn't want that. I wanted to be part of something that I chose, and gave my life some direction, instead of doing as my family wanted.

Eight months after I left for boot camp, I graduated ████ school. There, I learned a lot

But none of it would keep me off
of drugs and drinking.

I worked on an ambulance
~~from~~ for about four months while
waiting for the next college semester
to start. I made lots of
money and partied hard. Then
when I got into college, it got
worse. I had altered the course
of my life for a girl, who in
turn, left me for a rich boy,
then for a thug. That hurt
me, and I started partying
harder. I got very bad
off on crystal. Skipping class
and selling dope didn't really
work out. I still made pretty
good grades, but the college
told me that if I wanted
to continue with my schooling,
I'd have to behave like a
normal student. That wasn't
going to happen.

A few days after that
semester let out, I got orders
for deployment. I was so strung

out that I needed to be sent to Afghanistan to dry out. I was still high on the plane ride across the Atlantic Ocean.

I ended up being stationed in Pakistan. It was usually boring there. A few weeks after I got there the same girl broke up with me for the last time. Once again my way of dealing with my ~~since sense~~ feeling of loss was drinking and drugs. We made alchohol, I had access to pharmaceuticals, and could get opium from the locals. ~~Dg~~ Six months later I came home. I was to recieve a ████ Star, an award given for valorous actions and performance above and beyond. But I went wild when I got to America, and got caught by the Army. My punishment was not getting the ████ Star. They told me that I had to go to rehab or I would be kicked out of the Guard.

& I, having no intentions of quitting, found a way out. I went to a rehab facility, did the initial assesment, and got out of going. The lady who ga gave me the assesment wrote a reccomendation to the Army. In short, it said that rehab would do me more harm than good. It cost me $100 and a ███ Star to avoid trouble.

The next ten or so months I did nothing except work, crystal and cocaine. Manufacture came into the picture. My life revolved around alchohol, smoking crystal, shooting up cocaine, and seeing how many girls I could bring home. <u>At times I wanted my life to end.</u>

It was then that I had another opportunity to get my life straight. I managed to get a job at Camp ███ It was an active duty job with the National Guard. Exactly what

I needed at the time. I was broke and directionless. ~~My new job was~~ ████ at the Medical Clinic on post. Lots of money, paid for and furnished apartments, worked three days on and three days off. Life was good. I was drinking most every night, but drug free for about six months.

Eventually I was back to buying Sudafed in every store I went in. Life, back on crystal, was just the same as it was before, except I had more money to blow.

Several months down the road my best friend and partner in crime got busted. I just knew that they'd be looking for me. After that I was finished with crystal. Since then I've never cooked it and smoked/shot some twice. Being that close to prison still did not help get me under control.

I went back to the bars and drinking every night. Things were going better than they had been. I started dating one of my patients. She seemed nice enough. Even claimed to be a recovered addict, but since then I've been told that she wasn't really recovered, just hid it well. But that doesn't matter. We kept each other in check for a few months. One night we were drunk and gambling, and had a room at the casino. I convinced her to get high with me, for just one night. That didn't work out so well.

We both fell off into the hole of crack addiction. We both stopped paying our bills, spent all of our savings, went in debt, bounced checks, and sold almost everything we owned. Not long after she got busted by the Army. They

Sent her off to Army rehab, and left me unmolested.

I knew that something had to change, but couldn't stop smoking. My next great idea was to volunteer for a deployment to Iraq. It took almost six months to get to go, despite my continuous nagging of my command.

By the time I left, the girl and I had broken up and she had been shipped off to another Army rehab. I was stealing and pawning anything I could get my hands on. A friend of mine who is a Physicians Assistant got In trouble for writing me prescriptions for pain killers. He was sent away as well. The Army overlooked my problem because I was going to Iraq. My family and freinds were begging me to get off dope, but I didn't want to.

By the time I made it to Iraq I was in the worst shape ever. I found alchohol the first day, once I made it to my permanent base. Valium was found next. I remained sober during missions, but that was about the only time. After a few weeks of patroling missions, I had an opportunity to go to a much worse city. I jumped on the opportunity. Once there, I did everything I could, half way hoping I would get shot or blown up. Even volunteering for extra missions didn't help me get my wish.

When I got back to America I hit the ghetto and the bar wide open. After a few weeks ~~the~~ I knew it was time to get some help with kicking my addiction. I had spent all the money

I had saved in Iraq, and wasn't being allowed to work at the Medical Clinic anymore.

I asked the Army to send me to rehab. That request was discussed for a few days, then they sent me to Ft. ████ for one day. They gave me an assesment that said I needed to go to rehab. That sure took rocket science to determine.

I was supposed to go to rehab in Hattiesburg and live at Camp Shelby. This lasted three days. I was awakened one morning by my First Seargent and told to go outprocess. The commander had ~~determine~~ decided that ~~if~~ I wasn't their problem and that if I wanted rehab, I could pay for it and do it on my own time.

This angered me with life even more. I overdosed twice in the next six months. I worked on an oil rig that surely didn't help anything. During all of this I met a girl. My opinion is that she was the only thing that kept me hanging on to the idea of life.

I stole a thousand dollars from a very good Christian friend who had went out on a limb for me. Him and his wife took me into their home, trying to help me. In return I stole from them and jeprodized our friendship. Because of his forgiving personality, he is still one of my closest friends.

After I was kicked out of his house I was homeless for about five months. I

would usually spend all
of ~~the~~ money I made
offshore in the first few
days I was home. Then
stay with my girlfriend
for the rest of my
two weeks home.
    One night on the way
to work I didn't make
crew change. This was
actually the third month
in a row. I didn't even
call because I knew I
was fired. I was broke
and cracked out, plus my
car was messing up.
    With no where else left to go,
I went to the house of a
life long friend. I stayed and worked
with him for three weeks, until
I screwed him over too. ~~After~~
~~the~~ When I first got to his
house, him and his sister
helped me get signed up
at a Christian Recovery Center
But when I stole his

sisters car, I had to leave.

The next day my girlfriend took me to my Dad's house. I stayed there, helping family members out with odd jobs, in exchange for feeding me dinner. In less than two weeks I had a phone message from the Rehab Center   It was monday evening. I tried to call but the office was already closed. As my family expected I left home that night to get drunk and high, because in my mind, I was going to rehab the next day.

After sobering up the next day, I knew how wrong I was. In one night, I had dissapointed everyone who cares for me, stole + sold things that were not mine, got my dads truck stuck in a ditch. After that I stole a truck from some friends who were not home to pull dads truck out.

Later that day I called the Rehab Center. They had called the previous day just to make sure I was still coming the following Monday. I had freaked out and flew off the handle for no reason.

The next week I stayed at home, or with my Dad, and during that week, I knew what I had to do. The following Monday my wonderful, caring girlfriend brought me to the Rehab Center and dropped me off. Not backing out of this program was the second hardest choice I have ever made. Riding down the driveway to the Rehab Center, I knew I had come to the turning point of my life.

About five days later I made the hardest descision a

man can make. To humble
myself before Jesus, and ask
him into my heart that I
~~can~~ could live for him.
After making that descision
I can see how much torment
I have put myself and others
through; for no reason at all.
　　At this time in my life
I do not know what God has
in store for me. I don't
know if my role in the Kingdom
of God will be large or small,
but the one thing I do
know is that it means
something to God, and that
alone has given me happiness,
purpose, and reason to push
forward.

All I Had To Do Was Believe

Dear Hillfighters, my Testimony is probally
the same as a million others. I was born in
1963 and moved to mississippi in 1966, my
father was a alcholic, and I followed in his
footsteps, for the longest Time I was a
functiong drunk, I went to work everyday
raised a family, paid my bills on time. when
it got worse, I started missing work, not
spending time with my family or going to
church. eventually it landed me in jail
for domestic violence disturbing family peace.
after two months in jail they put me on
probation. I was back in charge or so I
thought. I kept drinking and doing all the things
I've always done, finally I lost my job and
was sleeping in my car. I didn't think it
could get any worse then it did again, I totalled
out my car just before christmas, I didn't know
what to do anymore. and just wanted to die.
then for some reason a voice told me to call
a old friend from church, thats when the
lord started blessing me, his family took me
in and he told me of a place that could
help me get on the right path. but I didn't
have the money, he told me to pray about
it and put it in the lords hands. the next
day my old pastor called and said he wanted
to talk to me. I didn't want to go at first,
I just knew I was going to be judged, but
I wasn't he told me god had a plan for me
and to confess my sin's to him, and I did
I cryied like a baby.

the next thing I know the Mission House called and told me, that the same people at my church I thought were judging me had raised the money to get me in. I've been here three weeks and each day my heart gets lighter & lighter, the joy of the lord's coming back to me slowly but surely. The lord has been waiting for me to take the first step towards him and he's come running, to me. even a old drunk is welcome in the lord's eyes. I now know that the lord has a plan for me and has blessed me. all it took was that first step towards him. Thank you for letting me share this with y'all. and may the lord bless y'all & keep y'all safe.

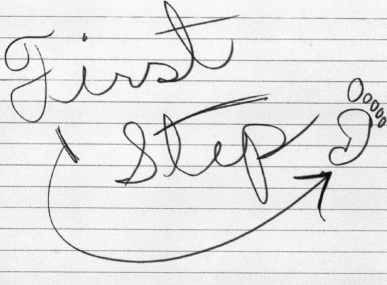

All My Family is Dead

My name is ~~⬛⬛⬛⬛⬛~~ and this is some of my story. I had a good childhood, I lived with my mother, father, older brother, grandmother and uncle, we all lived in the same house. I was a very happy child. My older brother got paralyzed when he was twelve but he stayed in high spirits, but this isn't about him. When I was about 11 my parents split up and that took a big toll on me. Me and my mom moved in with my brother which by this time had his own house, land and he had gotten married and got a college degree. When I was 12 my brother passed on and I found his body and I was devistated, he was my hero. My grandmother and uncle passed the same year on the same day, my grandma found my uncle which passed in his sleep and had a heart attack. I was young and hurt. I just gave up on school and myself. My father went to prison because he suffered a lot through that time too, and got in a lot of legal troubles, so it was just me and my mom. By this time I discovered what drugs was, Marijuana, pills, crystal meth. I really enjoyed these things because it was a temporary escape from reality, but it didn't stop the pain it just numbed it. By this time I was around 14 and had started working & my mother had gotten sick, her kidneys started failing. Unfortunately my drug use had gotten worse and I was getting in trouble, as well as my mom for not going to school. I blamed it on the drugs so I ended up in training school, Detention Centers and Rehabs but none of it helped. I would do good for a little while and go right back to the same ole "Eddie." Mine and my mom's relationship got very difficult because she wanted more for me.

It got so bad she even told me one time, she wished I would have died instead of my brother, I know she didn't mean it, it was just a ought of anger but I never will forget it. I met a girl when I was sixteen, she was 18 and unlike most kids my age I had a car a job and thought I knew everything and I could do it all on my own. She got pregnant and I got scared, but when my son was born it was like I was too, I was happy again in my life and I said I was going to straighten up and do right, well two weeks later my son passed away and I was crushed again, so back to the drugs I went, full speed ahead and I discovered crack and alchohal as well as the other stuff I was doing. The amount of drugs and alchohal I was doing at my age was unreal I had discovered needles as well. My mom had gotten sicker she had gotten put on dialysis and I was on a constant search for an escape from reality and pain. The loss of my son and my drug use drove me and my girlfriend apart. Well I was still working and I met another woman when I was about 18, she was 29 and had been married twice with 3 kids. She was in an abusive relationship, and I guess I thought I was going to be her savior but the truth was I couldn't even save myself but I tried and I got real attached to her kids and treated them as my own for almost 5 years, then once again my drug use and alchohalism split us up even though she did drugs too and me and my mother ended up with a "friend" of mine whose house got raided and seized for manufacturing meth. So we ended up in a hotel and I was still drinking and using more than ever, one night my mom told me to lay down with her and I smarted off to her and she hit me in my eye so I layed down.

Well I was the only one who woke up the next morning. I went crazy at first but then I realized she wasn't suffering anymore so I grabbed her cold hand and thanked the lord for that, kissed her forehead goodnight and helped the coroner load her body up, that was the last time I believe I felt the presence of the lord till a week ago. After all of that, i'm going to go ahead and sum it up because my heart is eager but my hand is tired, I lost my job, and became homeless and I thought my life was hopeless till I met an extraordinary individual ██████████ and he told me about this place and I believe the Lord brought him to me and me to Mission at the Cross. I have never felt this kind of Love in one place in my Life. I see Miraculous things in people everyday and the Lord is strong here. I'm surrounded by people like me and there is something here I can't even put in words but it is great and I just thank the Lord and Mr. ████████ for bringing me here. I have embraced the Lord and opened my heart and my eyes and I've only been here for 2 weeks. I am still at war everyday but instead of going to a straw, a bottle, a pill, or a needle when my struggles are seeming unbearable i've been going to my bible and it's the best high i've ever felt in my life, this is the happiest i've been in a very, very long time.

Thank You
Jesus !!!

All My Husbands Beat Me

Dear Pastors, Associates, & Friends,

My friend ████████ turned me on to your orginazation by wearing one of your T-Shirts and showing me your Bible. ████████████████████████████

I am a mid 50 year old twice married woman. Guess I was pretty nieave cause both times I thought I'd be married till death till we do part — I just didn't think that meant ████████ they had the right to kill me.

Husband #1 was an alcoholic which became obivious to me — (what wasn't so obvious to my 17 yr. old heart) was that he had become a Heroine Addict in the course of our 11 year marriage. Complete with physical abuse to me, running around with other woman, only working to supply his habits — while I not only worked but did double shifts in a nursing home, usually battered & bruised.

Husband #2 was pretty much a repeat of the 1st — First Alcohole but then he got involved with Crack Cocacaine. In my insanity I thought I would fix his wagon by going to work as a BARTENDER where as I could have him barred. You guessed it — More Beatings — More Woman

This time however I turned slightly even BADDER and had a couple of affairs in relateation. The final straw in that marriage was when he beat me into the Hospital (again) He went to Jail (again) but this time when I got out I took off with a man who brought me to the Guelf Coast.

For a 3d time he wasn't any better than the other 2 so after a stay @ the Salvation Army I turned

my life around, moved to ▓▓▓▓▓▓ MS - met
Jesus Christ my Personal Savior and live my life for
him and Father GOD.

There is no earthly man in my life but
thats alright - if and when the time is right Father
will provide but for the past 4 or 5 years I'm
content to live alone and live for GOD

Satan keeps throwing serious Health
problems @ me but thats O.K. because stronger is
He that is in me than that of the world and my
precious Jesus keeps takeing these infirmity's
away from me.

I am Happy & Healthy in the Joy of the Lord
Hallajeah & Amen
Sincerely
Your Sister in Christ

Can You Do It? Yes!

Praise God! What a long strange trip it's been. Way back when I was very young. I was shown the way in which I would live my life for the next 35 years. Before I start let me say, God's word says in Romans 8:28; "And we know that all things work together for good to them that love God, to them who are the called according to his purpose."

My story starts when I was 5, that's when my parents and their friends started physically and sexually abusing me. As I got older they would tell me this is what their lord liked. By the time I was 11, I come to learn of their lord (Satan).

Of coarse by this time I started doing to others what had been done too me. I ran away from home at age 13 never to return. At 16 I was some what adopted by a group of bikers out of Ohio.

Things did not get much better for me with them. I was still doing crazy things, by the time I was 18 this man, an ex-biker with the Hells Angels became my legal guardian. Dr. T▓▓, has been a Reverend for the Lord Jesus for over 30 years. Satan still had a very strong hold on me, and for many years Dr. J (dad), has tried to break that hold. Everybody tried many ways but it took coming to prison for God to get me to hear the knock his Son was placing at my door. It took time, but on June 13,   ; I opened my door to Jesus! It has been many years, but as time goes by my walk becomes easier.

I've learned how to truly forgive all those who harmed me. As well as all who took part in showing me the wrong things in my life. Jesus has shown me how to forgive myself, and how to love again, real love, not the love of the world.

There are still area's in my life that still need to be worked on. But as Paul says: "Being confident of this very thing, that he which hath begun a good work in you will perform it until the day of Jesus Christ:" Phill. 1:6. Thank you for hearing me out. Always remember: "...because greater is he that is in you, than he that is in the world."

I John 4:4

Cocaine Took Over My Life

Dear Hellfighters,

My name is ████████ I am 20 years old and currently staying at the ████ ████████ as a client. I was born in Mississippi on July ████ and grew up in Ocean Springs ███. I have one brother who is ██ years old and two great parents. Growning up I went to a Catholic Private School and even graduated from a Catholic High School. I went to church all my life. Around the age of 13 I started smoking cigarretess. A couple years later a friend of mine offered me some weed and I smoked it and liked the way it made me feel. That was when I was in 8th grade. I continued to use Marijuana and started drinking alkhol and taking pills around 11th grade. That was when my life started to get miserable and my grades and motivation went down. Two years out of high school (witch I managed to graduate just barely) I was attend a community colledge and I started using cocaine on the weekends with friends. I got addicted to the cocaine and it took over my life. I was using every day and it got so bad I had to drop out of school. I went to my Mom and told her I needed to get help. She heard about the ████████ through a friend and got me here. Now that I am here I realize I was using drugs and alkhool →

to fill a void in my heart. That void was that I did not have Jesus Christ. I went to church all my life but never really put him number 1. in my life. I could really use a KJV bible. I really appreciate what the Hellfighter people do, and what you people stand for. Thank You and may the Lord Bless You all.

GOD ROCKS !!

P.S. I want to give a special thanks to
          Romans 13:6

Crack is Like a Whirlwind

I have been an alcoholic/drug user since my early teen years. If I went drinking, I was smoking weed. I did this all through school and all my life up to now. I am 39. The longest time that I can remember being totally sober is 9 years ago when I found out I was having a baby — I stayed completely clean for 1½ years, then came the drinking, heavy. Everyone told me I was real bad, I would black-out but keep going. So I showed them, I started smoking crack, big time. This sin took over me like a whirlwind, I was out of control, I lost everything, even custody of my son and then my freedom. This happened on July 4th this past year, I got caught with crack and got a felony possession charge.

I spent 18 months in ▓▓▓▓▓ County Adult Dentention Center, and ~~while~~ there, I entered into a program called Life Skills a Bible based rehab/type setting, classes every day about how to live a moral Christian life by Biblical standards, and the program changed my life — I met God and now I have Him in my life. From HCADC, I came to this rehab center to double ensure my strength, and to gain more knowledge and wisdom for the rest of my recovery. I look forward to my new spiritual journey and can't wait to experience all the great mericals God has planned for me. I will continue my walk in total faith in Christ I know I have a ways to go. But, "I can do all things through Christ who strengthens me."

DO YOU REALLY LOVE HIM?

"She has done a good work for Me" (Mark 14:6).

If what we call love doesn't take us beyond ourselves, it is not really love. If we have the idea that love is characterized as cautious, wise, sensible, shrewd, and never taken to extremes, we have missed the true meaning. This may describe affection and it may bring us a warm feeling, but it is not a true and accurate description of love.

Have you ever been driven to do something for God not because you felt that it was useful or your duty to do so, or that there was anything in it for you, but simply because you love Him? Have you ever realized that you can give things to God that are of value to Him? Or are you just sitting around daydreaming about the greatness of His redemption, while neglecting all the things you could be doing for Him? I'm not referring to works which could be regarded as divine and miraculous, but ordinary, simple human things—things which would be evidence to God that you are totally surrendered to Him. Have you ever created what Mary of Bethany created in the heart of the Lord Jesus? "She has done a good work for Me."

There are times when it seems as if God watches to see if we will give Him even small gifts of surrender, just to show how genuine our love is for Him. To be surrendered to God is of more value than our personal holiness. Concern over our personal holiness causes us to focus our eyes on ourselves, and we become overly concerned about the way we walk and talk and look, out of fear of offending God. ". . . but perfect love casts out fear . . ." once we are surrendered to God (1 John 4:18). We should quit asking ourselves, "Am I of any use?" and accept the truth that we really are not of much use to Him. The issue is never of being of use, but of being of value to God Himself. Once we are totally surrendered to God, He will work through us all the time.

FEBRUARY 21

Dear

"You said you 'found God.' Does that mean you asked Jesus in your heart? If so, Praise God for your salvation. Because to get to the FATHER, we have to go thru the SON, Jn. 14:6.

Also, you ought to replace that word recovery with DELIVERANCE. A person in ICU is recovering from a problem, a person the instant they accept CHRIST, are 'a new creature'... II Cor. 5:17. "NOW the LORD is that SPIRIT: and where the SPIRIT of the LORD is, there is Liberty." FAITH. We believe, II Cor. 3:17.

[struck-through text] Write me sometime. I'm in prison. Robert Goldsmith

Rev. 21 Heaven

Daddy Did It, So Why Shouldn't I?

Hi. My name is ▓▓▓▓▓▓▓
I am twenty four years old. I am
from Cherokee, ▓▓. I have one child,
a boy whose named Dra▓e▓▓▓▓▓▓▓
▓▓▓▓. Draver is 2 yrs old. I
am a client at a Christian rehab
center in MS for the second time.

I became a drinker at the age
of 14 yrs old. I grew up in a small
town and small towns usually lead
to partying really hard and actually
trying to be "The life of the Party".
That's what I was for years. My
mom and Dad divorced when I was
in the second grade. My Dad was
an alcoholic and I thought drinking
was normal, I mean "Daddy did
it" so I thought it was okay. My
Daddy loved us and believe it or not
loved the Lord he talked about God
alot. I remember my Daddy would
drink for months and quit for
months. He would talk about God
drinking or not. I have a brother
named ▓▓▓▓▓ who is now 26 yrs
old and now he is in prison ▓▓

█████ in Montgomery, AL. █████
and I loved our Daddy alot and
Daddy loved us too but didn't
really show us the right way to
live. He showed us how to drink
and live. My daddy was disabled,
he got hurt on the job and couldn't
work any longer. My mom and
dad didn't live far apart so my
Dad still got and wanted to be a big
part of my life. My mom worked
alot, she has worked really hard
all of my life. I actually title
my mom as a "workaholic" and
that's okay. She always provided
for █████ and I. Momma loves
the Lord and we always attended
church as a child. My brother
was a hyper child which was diagnosed
with ADD and I was a quite child.
My mom started dating this man
named █████ when I was in
the eighth grade and I remember
starting to go out on the town
when my mom started going to
his house alot during the week

and she started spending the night
on the weekends. The party began
I drank on the weekends I can't
remember ever taking one off all
through High School and actually
drinking some during the week. I
found my boyfriend in High School his
name was ███████ we had lots of
good times in 2 yrs. He played
baseball and football ███████
always told me he would die on
a baseball field and he really did.
He was playing with some younger
players one evening, he jumped
over the fence when someone hit
the ball over, he grabbed the
fence and the light pole and the
light pole wasn't grounded and it
electrocuted him. ███████ died in the
hospital ███████. I was
devestated. I still drank alot. I
found another boyfriend about a
year later his name was ███████
and he was a big drinker himself
and while dating ███████ I get introduced
to marijuana, cocaine, oxy contin,

tried to run over the police. I shoplifted on a daily basis. I was then introduced to Cocaine. I had met my husband during this time. My husband drank alot. Later, I became pregnant with our son Drake who is 2█ yrs old now. I quit doing Cocaine, but did not give up doing pills while I was pregnant with ████████. By God's grace and I thank him everyday that Drake is a healthy child. Drake did have Colic and my husband ████ didn't enjoy all the crying. I started disliking ████ because he would not chelp. I started taking lots of pain killers. I well was then introduced to Crack. Crack is what really destroyed my life. My home, My family every thing was gone before I knew it. This is not only my second time here. This is my fifth rehabilitation in 3 yrs. God is restoring my family, day by day. I thank him everyday for bringing me here.

I have ~~XXX~~ been here ■ weeks.
I hope to learn alot while here
at the home

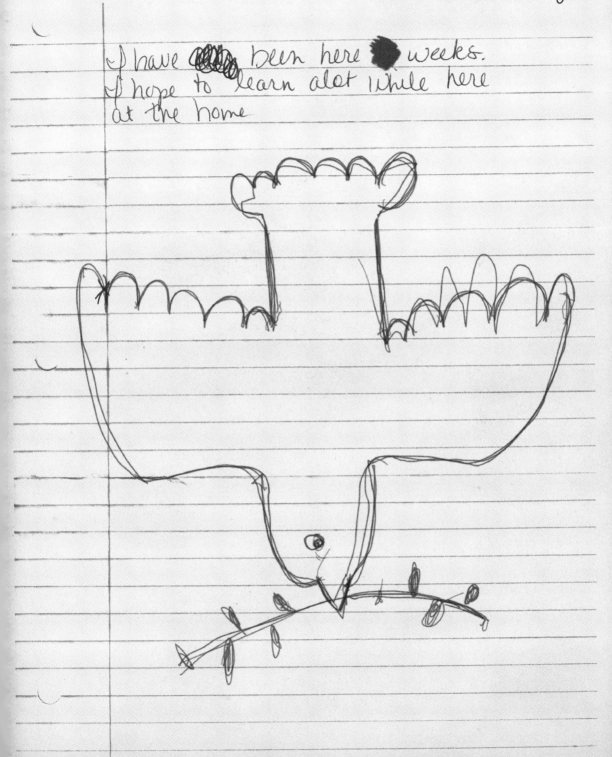

Does Anybody Really Care?

To whom it may concern;

Hello my name is ██████ ██████ I am currently incarcerated at the ██████ Unit in ██████ Tx. Texas Dept. of Criminal Justice. A friend of mine let me see his Search & Rescue Hand Book. I guess he saw I was giving up Hope & Faith. See I am from Pennsylvania. I have no family nor friends in Texas all my family & friends are in PA. Now, Aug 4th ██████ I lost my father then Aug 30th ██████ I lost my mother. I couldn't be there to say Good-Bue then June 4th ██████ my oldest brother passed away. My son has Down Syndrome & 3 holes in his heart & he has been granted his final wish thru make a wish foundation then my wife has severe nerve damage from her diabetes. & she has a heart murmur. They barely make it out there with out me, I keep praying & keep hoping something good will happen. I've begged god for mercy & I'm about to give up. I can't get myself to keep trying. I need help & every where I turn no one really cares. I talked to my buddy & he said ya'll have helped him. Well thank you for your time & hope to hear from ya'll if not I understand. Again thank you & may god bless you & your family.

RH's Note:
Gina & I wrote a book entitled America's Churches Through the Eyes of a Bum and published it in 2012. It speaks about the lack of concern sweeping America. WE CAN ALL DO BETTER - CAN'T WE! And we should.

To My BROTHERS IN CHRIST!

My NAME ████████████
I WAS BORN IN 1971 AT
CABRINI HOSPITAL IN ALEXANDRIA
LOUISIANA. MY MOM AND DAD MET
IN VIETNAM IN 1967. DAD WAS
A BIKER W/ the HELL's ANGELS ████
████ IN CALIFORNIA. WE MOVED
BACK TO LOUISIANA WHEN I WAS
FIVE. GREW UP IN ████████ LA.
LEFT WHEN I GRADUATED HIGH
SCHOOL IN ██. MOVED To SEATTLE
WITH MY FIRST WIFE AND
BEGAN To LIVE what I thought
WAS the "AMERICAN DREAM".
GOOD JOB, NICE HOUSE, PARTIES
ON the WEEKENDS????
DIVORCED IN ██ AND BEGAN TO
REALLY LIVE the "SINGLE LIFE"
GREW AND SOLD ALOT OF WEED. BOUGHT
METH FROM A MAN IN A BOAT FROM
SAN DIEGO EVERY OTHER WEEKEND
AT THE HARBOR. SOLD AND USED
METH FOR OVER 2 YEARS, NONSTOP.
████████ ENDED UP BACK IN LA.
ALEXANDRIA OF COURSE!

BUILDING AIRPLANES AT A NEW
REPAIR STATION THAT HAD
JUST OPENED. MET MY WIFE
THERE AND IN 98' WE HAD
▓▓▓▓▓ MY FIRST CHILD, HER
SECOND. AT THAT TIME I REALIZED
THAT AVIATION AND COCAINE WERE
MY WHOLE LIFE. BEGAN SMOKING
CRACK AND 8 YEARS LATER I'm
AT A Christian Recovery Center WE
TRAVELED ALOT WITH MY JOB
WE BEING MY WIFE ▓▓▓▓, OUR
OLDEST BOY ▓▓▓▓, AND THE YOUNGEST
▓▓▓▓▓▓ I PUT THEM THROUGH
PURE HELL FOR MANY YEARS.
MAKING ALOT OF MONEY AND
SPENDING IT TOO! WE MOVED
TO ▓▓▓▓▓▓▓▓▓. IN ▓▓▓▓
FOR A 757 BOEING
CONTRACT THAT I TOOK FROM
SEATTLE. SO WE SETTLED
IN, AND I THOUGHT, "HERE'S
MY CHANCE TO START FRESH!
WENT TO MOBILE AEROSPACE
AND STARTED THIS HUGE
PROJECT. everything was going
PRETTY GOOD.

THEN I FOUND A GROUP OF GUYS TO DRINK WITH EVERYDAY! AND THEN I FOUND CRACK AGAIN.

MY WIFE AND children STARTED GOING TO CHURCH IN DAPHNE AND WERE DRAWING CLOSE TO GOD, MEANWHILE I STAYED AT WORK OR HIGH MOST OF THE TIME.

EVENTUALLY I GAVE IN TO JESUS CALLING ME, AND STARTED ATTENDING church ALSO. GOT SAVED ▪▪▪ AMEN! BUT!

RODE THE FENCE FOR A COUPLE OF YEARS. VERY PAINFUL!

RAN MY WIFE AND KIDS OFF! THEY WERE STAYING WITH A FRIEND FROM church while I SELF DESTRUCTED.

THEN JESUS SHOW HIMSELF TO ME, while

I LAY CRYING ON THE FLOOR OF MY HOUSE ALL ALONE, COMING DONE OFF OF 3 OR 4 DAYS OF CRACK.

HE HEARD MY CRY AND SAID TO ME! I'M HERE!

IT WAS A MOMENT I'll NEVER FORGET. BUT! I STILL TURNED MY BACK ON HIM AFTER I GOT MY FAMILY BACK AND ██████ AND I GOT MARRIED I STARTED SMOKING CRACK AGAIN. PURE HELL!

STARTED A CONSTRUCTION BUSINESS, DID WELL! MY CHURCH, WIFE, AND MOM PRAYED ME INTO THIS Wonderful Recovery Center PUT DOWN CIGARETTES AFTER 21 YEARS OF SMOKING!

I HAVE JESUS IN MY HEART NOW PRAISE GOD!

I GRADUATE ON JUNE 2ND
AND I'm SO READY FOR GOD
TO BE my FRIEND my SUPPORT
AND my WAY.

HE HAS SAVED my LIFE! my
MARRIAGE, my CHILDREN
AND I LOVE HIM WITH
ALL THAT I AM.
I PRAISE HIS GREAT
WORK IN ME AND I WILL
LEAVE HERE AND WAIT FOR
HIM TO TELL ME my MINISTRY.

ONE OF YOUR GUYS CAME TO
CHAPEL THE OTHER
NIGHT AND GAVE YOUR TESTIMONY!
THANK YOU! THAT WAS S
AWESOME.

GOD BLESS
YOU

CHRIST'S
OWNED
ROGER

Drugs Are Strong, But
God is Stronger

Hellfighters,

I'm writting because,
my little Brother ▮▮▮▮ who is at ▮▮▮▮ Eightyeins
▮▮▮▮ Recovery in Chunky,
MS. gave me your
address & wanted me to
write & tell my testimony
about how God has
changed my life.

My name is ▮▮▮▮ I live in
▮▮▮▮ Alabama
always have! Although
I've never been addicted
to Drugs it seems like
every pickup in my life
& around me has been!

My family which
was my Mother, Father
& three Brothers was
always strong! My
God, Mother & Father
made sure of that! the
strength was in the
Bible & as my Dad would
say "Old School way"
That was our Childhood
then came along
adult hood. The Devil
set in & God's shield

fall down."

My Oldest Brother. ~~____~~ "Abused "Alcohol & Crack Cocaine for over fifteen years." Then married "An Addict of anything & everything." his addiction Consumed my life for over fourteen years. Well, not only mine but two precious Daughters!

My Brother ~~_____~~ used "Crack Cocaine until it ended his Life." I prayed all the time for my family! Nothing but Changed. Then one day I received a call early Saturday Morning at work my younger brother was found shot in his head dead.

~~ooo~~ my Brother was 25 years old. Left two Children me, ~~_____~~ Mom Dad & our Oldest Brother. I grieved could not understand "God's reason for his Death". Everything was still the same nothing changed! Except my brother was gone, that was not the prayer I wanted answered.

████████ my Oldest Brother, my Ex-husband (now) Cousins, friends & so on kept on using "Crack Cocaine"

But, Believe it or not one year later my Oldest Brother "stopped" completely. Clean clear I thank God every day for his grace.

████████ HE is at a wonderful Recovery Center getting off Crack Cocaine. He got saved & Baptized! Thank you God.

Finally after fourteen years off battling Gambling, Drug & so on with my Husband I had to break free. The girls & myself are doing better than ever before God showed me the way.

God also sent me someone in my life from my childhood and recently got engaged Christmas this year! My testimony may not be one of the worst you've heard but to me it was because it was my life & I lived it everyday. God & prayer helped me thru everyday.

I lost one I loved but God saved the other!

Addictions are strong but God, prayer & faith is stronger.

Hellfighter
always & forever

Everything Went To Hell

Dear Hellfighters,

My name is ███████████. I was born ██████, in ██████. I had an awesome childhood. Got to travel, played sports. I was an all american kid. Always had everything I ever wanted and more. My father died Christmas Eve ████, I was 16. Well after he died I started drinking on the weekends. My buddies and I would go to my parents lake house and throw down. In ██ I graduated from a small private christian school, moved to Tusc. AL to attend University of Alabama. That is when things really started going down hill. I started going out to the bars, raves, and any other parties I could find. I started doing exstacy, Meth, GHB, cokes, anything I got my hands on. I never got addicted then. I could use for months and stop for months. My parents found out ████ and moved me home. I stayed straight for awhile. Went back to school in "03". Started going to phrat parties & more bars & raves. I graduated in spring of ████. One night while I was out drinking with my cousin. She asked if I wanted to do a pill. I said sure. I didn't realize at this time I was about to start using neddles. After that everything went to Hell. I was main lining everyday. I ~~spent~~ 300,000 dollars in less than 2 years, must fund left by my
from a

Dad. I also started stealing. I stole over a 100,000 dollars from my grandparents. I was writing checks of their account. I was also charging thousands of dollars on credit cards they paid for. They didn't press charges until I did ~~~~ the check thing for the third time. So my mother decided to send me to a christian rehab. I really didn't want to be here but, I've made the best of it and God is really working in my life. I look forward to having my life back.

Yours in Christ,

RH's Note:
It's evident that this young man has not turned his life over to Christ, BUT... he's making an HONEST EFFORT and without an HONEST EFFORT true change will never come.

I would also like information on how to purchase Satan Sucks shirts. Size L

God is Good!

Dear Brothers & Sisters in Christ,

God is so awesome! Let me introduce myself and give ya'll my testimony of how God's worked in my life. My name is ██████████, but people call me ████. Im 22 years old and am currently in ██████ County Detention Center in ██████, ██████.

For the most part I was raised in a Godly Family. When I was about 5 or 6 my parents divorced. I dont really remember too much about it. My mom re-married when I was 9 or 10. I didnt like my new step dad too much but he made my mom happy and thats all that matterd. My Dad wasnt really there for me until I become a teenager. That had an effect on my life. When I was 11 years old, I was sexually molested by a Family "Friend". That tormented me growing up so much. By the time I was 17 I had done almost every drug there is. I got kicked out of a private school and startin runnin the streets. In March ██ I went to jail for selling my step-dads four-wheeler for drug money. The judge sent me to a home for troubled teens for 2 years or until I ~~was~~ graduated high school. After a year later I was sent to jail for Assault & Battery High Aggravated Nature. I bailed out and went back home to ██████ nc, this was May ██ By November ██ I was addicted to crack cocaine. At the time, it was my life. January ██ I was admitted in a hospital for trying to kill myself. Rehabs wouldnt work. I tried

3 different ones. Two months later I went to court my my Assault charge. The Judge sentenced me 1-6 years in prison. It was then that I asked God to change me. To take over my life. I tried it my way and look where it got me. I asked Him to come in my life and to please Forgive me for my wrong. During my time in prison I grew so close to God and was finally truelly happy for once. I got out ~~████~~ (14 months later). I served God when I came home but then I got weak and started slacking off in my prayers and Bible study. ~~Eventully the devil took hold of my life.~~ I decided to come to a Noscar Race here in ~~████████~~ I got locked back up that night. This is what it took to bring me back to God. I didnt do what Im charged with and God knows it but I feel like this was His will for me. I started reading the Word again and saw in John 14:14 that we can receive what we ask for as long as we believe. So I said "God, please dont let me go back to prison." And I believe it. Later He told me in Acts that Im going to go home after I go to court. (Acts 16:36 - "The magistrates have sent to let you go. Now therefore depart, and go in peace."). He told me yet again in Nahum that Im not goin back to prison (Nahum 1:9 - "... affliction shall not rise up the second time.") So I know beyond a shadow of doubt Im not goin back to prison. I read in Matthew

one day that if 2 agree here on earth concerning anything we ask, God'll do it. I said to my friend: "████████, lets agree when we pray that ya'll go home by next week and when I go to court my charges'll be dropped and I'll be going home" So we did. Two days later ████████ went home, they gave him time served. The very next day my lawyers came to tell me that the solicitor saw I passed the polygraph and is in the process of dropping my charges! Praise God! He is so good to us. So I tell everyone (while I wait to go to court) that Gods goin to make a way for me to go home. God spoke to me again in Romans 3:4-"you will be proved right in what you say, and you will win your case in court." It cont get any clearer than that. He is so merciful and graceful. Im still waiting to go to court. It keeps getting continued but I know that Gods on my side and that Im going home! I believe God wants me to be a youth minister when I come home (2 Corinthians 1:3-5), because I can relate to teens.

I saw ya'lls NIV new testament Bible and was wondering if I could please get one. I'd like it to carry around with me in my pocket and witness to others. If it costs anything I'll be happy to send money. If yall have any other literature I can better myself with, I'd love that & also. I completely understand if Im asking for too much tho.

Thank you so much for your time. I will be praying for your ministry. Please pray for me. May God bless you with His goodness and riches. If it wasn't for Him we'd have no reason to live. Thanks again

Psalms 50:15

Half a Pill Almost Took My Life

Dear Hellfighters,

     I am writing to give you my testimony about how I came to know Jesus. I have been addicted to drugs for the past nine years. I am 25, and started when I was sixteen. I started like most other addicts do with marijuna and alcohol. My sister and me smoked a joint behind my dad's tool shed for the first time when I was sixteen she was 19. My addicition grew bigger and badder when me and my friend decided to try some extasy at a club one night. We both split one pill and by the end of the night I thought that it was the best night of my life, and I had finally found what I was looking for. With the drug I could have all the women (that did the drug I wanted) Little did I know the truth was it would destroy and change my life for the next seven years. I started to get into the drug hard so I decided I should sell it. I meet a guy that supply it at a cheap prices and I had people that wanted it. I started selling in local clubs and to my friends. As I started to get deeper bigger and more drugs came. I started experimenting and selling L.S.D, Cocaine, Special k, Xanex, methaphimine. As the drugs kept coming in so did the women, money, and partys. I really thought I was living it up. I started to party to much, and I violated the probation I was on, and I warrent was put out for my arrest. I was facing two and a half years in prison. I lived on the run for the next six months. Everything was going wrong I picked

two new drug possesion charges luckily not
traffiking charges and bonded out. I stay on
the run. I did not turn myself in, because
I thought I was in love with this girl
that really did'nt even care about me she
just cared about partying. Finally one night
my friend got caught selling drugs, and he
quickly rated me out. told them where I was.
They arrested me, and that would be all the
partying I would do for the next 2½ years.
The girl I was with stay with me for six
month and then found another man. I + was just
lust and not love. I went from county to county
to get sentence to my three felony charges. They tried
to put me in Rehab. I went for a week, but
thought it was better to do the time, and get
it over with then have to do the Rehab and
probation afterwards. I finally got out in
~~██████████~~ I told myself I was not
going to go back to doing drugs, ~~but I would~~
smoke weed and drink a little bit. I started
working at a ~~███████████~~ waiting tables.
I was smoking pot everyday and drinking on
the weekends. One day I meet back up with
an old friend of mine, and he told me he could
get meth at a really good price. So I thought
well I can sell it at work, because all
the people at work did it, and not do any. A
bout two weeks later I started using again, and
after that I had a habit everyday for the
next 11 months. This time was a lot worse
then the last. I eventually quite my job, because

I really wanted to party. I started robbing and
stealing to support my habit. My life was really going
down the drain and every buck to prison or death. My
sister had came to know Jesus a year before
I got out of prison, and about six months ago
was really telling me I should get help. I
did not listen, because I was thinking I could
make it on my own. She continue to pray for me.
When Christmas came around all my money was gone.
All my so called friends left and I was really
getting sick of the drugs. I had a thought in my
head and told myself where I am going in my
life. I decided to stop and find help, I called
my sister and told her I wanted help, She got
me a bus ticket to a lady that would take care
of me be until I could find a rehab. I
missed my bus and had to wait 8 hours until the next
one came. I had twelve dollars my aunt had given
me and I decided to get drunk. I found a
bar and spent all my money. I was in the same
situation I had just come out of. So at that
moment I decided to quite. Gwite every thing
it was over I had enough. I got on my bus
and it was late at night. I was hungrey and had
no money. I sat down next to a guy who intro
duced himself to me. We talked and come to find
out he had 4 pounds of meth in his Jacket.
I was confused and frighten. Here I am trying
to get away from the drug I had just got
off. He asked me if I wanted a line. At
that moment I knew something was not
right. Now I know it was the devil trying

keep me from knowing the truth in Jesus. I started
sweating and this pull came upon me. I told him
no that I was through with drugs. I got
to ████ house and the next night I went to
a bible based 10 step program called the most excellent
way. I got saved, and the guy that help me
meet Jesus sponsored me to come to this Christian
Recovery Center The past month ████████
████ living with Jesus has
been the best in my life I have stop
smoking and all drugs my life is changing
and I feel a hundred times better about
my self. I look forward to living the
rest of my life growing to know Christ.
It is a daily walk, and the old me starts
to come back up sometimes. With the word
and prayer I know I will over it, I
am in need of a new bible if you could send
one, I heard you also give shirts when we
graduate. My size is large, I graduate
April ████. I thank you and pray for the
good things the Hellfighters are doing. I
ask you'll to keep me in you'lls prays,
God bless

Brother in Christ,

D

Half Breed

First I would like to thank you so much for the bible & scripture. My name is ▬▬▬▬▬▬▬▬ I read the storys inside and especialey yours. I enjoyed know that people other than myself are dealing with drug addiction & winning the fight with gods armor on.

About me..... I'm ½ white ½ mexican my dad was from Callifonia chapter of hells angels he was also a drug dealr & theif. I dont know much more than that. my mom was an recovoring drug user and became sick when I was a teenager she had leukeima and died at age 42 on her birthday I was 19 and had alreay had one baby at 17 and was heavlie useing Drugs. I was in a bed way and mad at god. my grandpa died shortley after my mom on fathers day. he was like my dad. I loved him. The family fell apart I had another baby I had given the fist one to my aunt and uncle. My seond was with a diffrent dad he had beat me & went to prison I got away from him. Then my grandma & another aunt took care of my seond child. I met a guy who I thought I would marry his dad was a preacher but his dad had beat his mom so bad that he decided that if that was god he wanted No part of it. I came to believe what he was saying I went to Jail about 11 mo after I had said I would marry him I was in CO Jail for 3 mo and he got another girl pregnat. Once I got I out I didnt know about her and we resumed our relationshi. I got Pregnat a third time, I finley felt I belonged when I found out the other girl was pregnant he decided to merry her because I found out he raped his sister & I left him. My first baby's dad turned out he wanted to be gay & left me for a guy. after all this I decide to sell drugs to be able to afford my addiction I had given my third child to a cousion & her husbnd they couldnt have children I still get to see all my kids. I was lost I stole some cars & got cought. also got arrested with drugs. the mothers day of 2008 I went to church for the fist time in years. I asked god to take me away from this life. shortley after the guy I was drugging with beat me and I ran. witch lead to me getting arrested a few days later. I was so fired but for the First time I saw things Clearley. I thanked god.

hear I am in prison & thanking god.
I got saved in Co. Jail and ended
up in a work release program then I
Back slid a bit and got in some
trouble I was sent to a max prison
wher I am now learining that god
is #1 in my life. It was so hard
to surrender to him I kept falling back
into old ways & habbits but I see
that full surrender is the only way
into true fullfilment. I'm into programs
& church now & have done a 360
from where I was. I'm still a
sinner but each day I grow and
am becoming more christlike. I
want to spiritualy mature and beome
what god planed for me to be. the
only way I can do this it to make
the right decisons & rebuke satan.
thank you for being such a wonderful
speaker of gods word 1st timothy 4:12
I believe you make a diffrence here
and you are a tree brother in christ.
I also want to thank you for writing to
me and each person who ~~loord~~ writes
you I find that extreamly extrotinary!
You are dedicated and I am so
glad you took the time to read my
story. here is a poem I wrote

Reverse side.

Guiding Light

A guiding light is what I need.
A tum to shead my tears of greif.
O Lord you say it's not easy.
I hide the pain ....
let the devil in again.
Realize what I have done.
Noteing that my souls been stung.
Repeating to the lord at night.
Emotionless by day I fight.
Anger, hate, terror strife.
Stabbs at my heart like a knife.
I look to god for peace of mind
his gentle hand so worm and kind.
This world, my life, all his designe.
That's how I know he is devine.
and like a star ahead he shines,
a guiding light, the lord is mine.

He Left Me For Dead

My NAME IS ████████ I Am
from ██████ Miss I Am THirty five years old
I Am Currently A student At A great Christian
Recovery Center. I HAve Just Recently excepted
(Jesus CHRIST) into My Life. I would Like to
explaine A Little Bit About Myself. I Came from
A Broken Home. Drinking Druging Soforth, I
found Myself excepting And Hunting THe wrong Kind
of friends. Well Sureley enough I Made My
way into THe drug world. I Never went to
Church As A Child, Never picked up A bible, never
New Jesus Christ, My drug use Started As.
Most A Little pot, And Acid, At 14 + 15. And
gradually Moved on with THe wicked Cycle of
Addiction until I found Myself Cooking Meth at
25 until one Night one of My So called
friends Came into My Home And Shot Me THree
times + Robbed Me + Left Me for dead.
THis was THE first Time god came into My life
And I didn't except Him. I Laid in The Hospital
for 5 Months in 90-90 Skeletal Traction, THis
is THe Time I was Introduced To Strong
pain Killers Lying in THat Hospital Oxy Cotin
Became My god you would THink Some one
Would Learn But no NoT Me when I
got out everything went right Back THe way
it was except I Had A new Addiction

To Add To My List. I went right Back to Cooking, THen one day Here Come tHe police And you Already Know THe rest, And get This it Still wasn't enough I got out of prison And went right Back to My old ways until one day THe Lord decided to Bless Me with A Little girl, ██████████████████ She was Born on ██████ And THis was THe Begining of THe end for Me THings Became So Much More to Me Looking into THe eyes of ██ My Baby girl. THen one day out of nowhere one of Mine And ████████ Mother Friends ████████ Started telling us About Jesus CHrist, And THis Begun the Movement That would Change our Lives forever, Now I Have A father A wonderfull forgiving father, My Light in All darkness. My Sheild Against Evil, ████████ And I decided to go into A Christian Program I Came to this Place And SHe went to another rehab we went on the same day god is working in My Life Shay was Saved Last Sunday Amen Now we Can Be THe parents our daughter deserves, I was Told you would wright Me Some encouraging THings And Maybe send Me A bible

I Really Need A good Bible THANK You for everything

IN CHrist

He Made It, But I Sold It

Hello. My name is ████████ I am 28 yrs old.
I am at a christian based Recovery Center
I started doing drugs when I was 15. Basically I
was just drinking on the weekends in 8th grade.
Soon I was smokings pot and skiping school. By
tenth grade I had missed 72 days the first semester,
and ended up quiting. I went back for my second
year in 10th, and ending up quiting it too. So, at
age 17 after quiting School I starting doing cocaine,
ecstacy twice. Then came meth which would take
controll off my life because I let it. At that time
I was dating a guy whos mom was penacostal. I
want to stop the drugs so I began going to cheerch.
Soon I was baptized at there church for my second
time. I was baptized at 12 at a baptist church but
really didn't no what I was doing then so I rededicated at
the penacostal cheurch. I recieved the holy spirit and
felt great. Not long after I was back sliding back to
meth + met who would be my sons father but
we were just friends then. I staying doing meth
every weekend untill we became a couple in 2000
He made meth and I sold it for him and did it every
day. I got very distant from my family and the lord
was tuging at my heart to get right. Of coarse he
did not like the fact that I wanted to change him

For two more years I stayed with him and he would hit me all the time. I loved him so much I thought I could change him. He would curse God for everything in his life, and I would pray for him. In ▮▮▮▮ I got pregnant, had an abortion and then got pregnant again. ▮▮▮▮ I gave birth two my son and was sober. ▮▮▮▮ His father, my fiance died of a heart attack at age 31. I continued on what I thought was a sober path for 2 more years. I was still drinking. I was working and got my Ged + started Cosmetology school and graduated ▮▮▮▮. Then meth came back into my life. So, I would spend alot of time away from my son and family who kept him when I was gone. I was in a really dark place. Then I met the boyfriend I have now. He made me happy and I was sober again. for about 6 months and start meth again behind his back and soon I was drinking every night to hide the fack I was high on meth. So, the lord started on my concous + heart again, And now I am here at this Recovery Center and I am really ready and have started giving it all to him.

"I can do all things through Christ who strengthens me"
  Phillipians 4:13   Thanks

He Paid Me With Pills

My name is ███████. I am 19 years old.
I was born on ████████████████.
I am from ████████, Louisiana,
born and raised. When I was
about 3 years old my parents and
I moved to ████████████ about 10
minutes away from Baton Rouge.
I met some friends in my neighborhood when I first moved there,
they were my age, two girls
████████████ and ████████. I started going
to church w/ them at the age
of 4. We attended ████████████
Baptist church in Baton Rouge.
I went to church and continued
to go to sunday school and vacation
bible school untill the age of 13 or
14. At the age of ███ 12 or 13
███████████ we went to this play
called "Heavens gates and hells
flames. I remember crying, I just
really felt the Holy spirit that
night. Well around 13 or 14 I
started highschool. I started to
hang out w/ all of the wrong
people, quit going to church.
It's like I lost God so quick
but never realized it. I started
off smoking pot on the weekends
then it became daily,

then I got introduced to pills. I met this 57 year old man, that had 3 babies 2, 3, and 4 years old, all girls. They were from New Orleans, and moved to (where I live.) they moved because of the hurricane. Well thats when my life went downhill. This guy went to the pain management clinic and got oxycotton, loratabs, somas, xanax, methadone. So I started to take all of that. I started off babysitting for him, and he paid me w/ pills. a year after all of this going on one day I had taken way more stuff than I should have. I took a bunch of methadone, and mixed it w/ xanax. I was knoddin out and kept falling asleep while I was walking and talking. I almost had an overdose. So after that, I got away from this guy and did good for a little while untill he showed up @ my house one day, he was telling me how much him and the kids missed me so I went back.

I ♥ you

His wife and kids mother
was in jail this whole time,
because of his murder charge.
She took the wrap for him
because someone overdosed on
his pills. well anyways his
kids ended up calling me
  momma, and i moved in
w/ him. I was taking pills
everyday for about two years
 untill i realized I needed help
and that wasnt the lifestyle
for me. I dont have any
kids so why should i have to
take care of someone else's
just for pills. I went to detox
and asked my probation
officer what rehab i could
go to, he mentioned the
local recovery center and thats where
I am now. I found God
 , ive been here for about
a month 3 a half.
            im happier than
ever. I would love to recieve
a bible and a t-shirt from
you guys. If yall have any
daily devotional books that
would be great, i need one.
Thank yall.

How Can I Keep My Sanity?

Dear Hellfighter,

Hello, my name is ███████ ████████. I am a 46 yr old white female currently incarcerated at the ████████ County Jail in ████████ Ms. One of my roommates gave me yall's address cause I was reading the little bible you guys had sent her and some of the testamonies I read were awesome. I would like for yall to pray for me and my children + my 88 yr old Mama who's in a nursing home. I am so lost right now. My charge is sale of a controlled substance to a C.I. It blows my mind. I lost my child, my car, my home and I don't even know which way to go. My children which are 3 girls 21, 19, 13 don't know what to do for me, they have never been through anything like this. We just need a lot of prayer and maybe some one could write and tell me how I can maintain my sanity and

try not to worry so much.
could you also send me some
litature so I can read about
the blessing's that God has bestowed
on others. I would deeply
appreciate it. thank you
you takeing the time to read
my letter.

      May God Bless You

      Sincerly

I Blew It All!

Hellfighters

Hello. My name is ████████ I'm 40
years old. I was saved at 11 years old. at
16 trying to fit in I started smokeing pot.
which lead into pornography, and drinking
at 21 years old. handsom and with the ability to
~~talk~~ Talk (gift of gab) in my 20's it was one
woman after the other lots of drinking, weed and
sex, exspirimenting with other drugs along the way.
Coke a few times, acid, hash, Crystal sold pot
for a few years. had good Job + lots of money.
At 30 smoked crack for the second time 1st
time was 2 years earlier. But the second time the
addiction to it kicked in, meat a girl few
months later got married 2 years later.
hid crack from her she doesn't do drugs or
w/pot. But doesn't like it. from ████████ old starting
to ██ years old at ███████████
Crack has almost destroyed everthing in my life
I'm Blessed By god to still have my wife +
2 Boys. 5 years old + 3 years old. we had car wreck
got $150,000.00 Blew it. got $274,000.00 for in herdance
Blew it. recently stole something got a Bugler
charge. No court date yet comes up this year.
I have a good Job. I'm a Floor Installer Been

Working for myself for 3 years. Made a lot
of Money. Blew it all. Had a Nice home
it Washed away in storm, No Insurance. But
Made a Bunch of Money Since storm But Blew
all of it. drugs have Controled Me for years

But I found a Cure.

Lord & Master I've Redicated My Life to
Christ. And I Live For him Now he is Number
1 in my life, I've turned all of My Life over
to him. Me, My Kids, My Marriage, where I
go, what i do. It's all in Jesus hand. I Love
him & praise him. I Can't wait to See what he
has in store the Next 20 years. of My Life.

                    Love you in Christ

① Could I have a Bible Please?

③ Would you, your Church, and the HellFighters
pray for me & Family and up coming, ~~people~~ Court Charges
I've Never been so Jail. I don't want to start
Now.

Dear

You found the only
cure for all our needs,
JESUS. He is al-
ways there for us,
Heb. 13:5&6. You
keep Him #1 in your
life, Matt. 6:33. Listen
to Him, Is. 30:21 & He will
guide you, Ps. 16:11. ☺
Write me anytime.
Love in Christ, Robert A. Smith
Micah 7:19   Matt. 10:21 Ps. 147:3

I Could Not Stop Drinking

My name is ██████████ and I'm from ██████, La. I'm currently at the Recovery center doing a 13 week drug abuse program. I'm 54 yrs. old and I am divorced.

I've had a drinking problem for years, but after my divorce in ████ things got a lot worse. Before my divorce I could handle my drinking to a certain degree, but after the divorce things got out of control. I started drinking on my job and missing work often. I worked for the ████ for 28 years, but drinking put an end to my career. I was lucky that the administrative staff gave me the option of taking an early disability retirement due to my poor vision and health problems. At least I have a steady income every month. But the cut in pay was drastic and hard to cope with. Also, all the idle time only made things worse.

(over)

I was very bored, so I applied for a part time job with the school board as a substitute teacher. Because I had a ▓▓▓▓ degree in Science and 28 yrs. of professional working experience, the school board hired me right away. I really liked teaching and I thought my life was going to turn around. But again, alcohol and drugs soon ended my teaching career.

Things got so bad that I lost my car, my apartment, and finally my health. I was staying in trouble with the law, constantly. To make a long story short, alcohol and drugs has just about destroyed my life. But I know it's not too late to pick-up the pieces. God will make sure of that.

Hopefully, This Recovery facilty will give me what I really need to try and put my life back together. It's got to be a step in the right direction.

RH's Note: Rehab alone won't fix the problem! But Jesus is the "Sure Fire" cure.

" Then was Jesus led up of the Spirit into the wilderness to be tempted of the devil."—Matthew iv. 1.

A HOLY character does not avert temptation—Jesus was tempted. When Satan tempts us, his sparks fall upon tinder; but in Christ's case, it was like striking sparks on water; yet the enemy continued his evil work. Now, if the devil goes on striking when there is no result, how much more will he do it when he knows what inflammable stuff our hearts are made of! Though you become greatly sanctified by the Holy Ghost, expect that the great dog of hell will bark at you still. In the haunts of men we expect to be tempted, but even seclusion will not guard us from the same trial. Jesus Christ was led away from human society into the wilderness, and was tempted of the devil. Solitude has its charms and its benefits, and may be useful in checking the lust of the eye and the pride of life; but the devil will follow us into the most lovely retreats. Do not suppose that it is only the worldly-minded who have dreadful thoughts and blasphemous temptations, for even spiritual-minded persons endure the same; and in the holiest position we may suffer the darkest temptation. The utmost consecration of spirit will not insure you against Satanic temptation. Christ was consecrated through and through. It was His meat and drink to do the will of Him that sent Him: and yet He was tempted! Your hearts may glow with a seraphic flame of love to Jesus, and yet the devil will try to bring you down to Laodicean lukewarmness. If you will tell me when God permits a Christian to lay aside his armour, I will tell you when Satan has left off temptation. Like the old knights in war time, we must sleep with helmet and breastplate buckled on, for the arch-deceiver will seize our first unguarded hour to make us his prey. The Lord keep us watchful in all seasons, and give us a final escape from the jaw of the lion and the paw of the bear.

Dear

No matter how close we get to the Lord, the temptations will be there, I Pt. 4:12, II Pt. 2:9, Ps. 34:17, I Cor. 10:13. The demons will hound you, Eph. 6, Ps. 18:1-3, 17, 48, 23:4, and God is on your side, Heb. 13:5,6, Is. 49:16, Phil. 4:13, II Tim. 1:7, NO FEAR. Write me anytime. Been There, Done That. Love in Christ, Robert A. Smith

matt. 6:21, Ps. 147:3

I Couldn't Do Anything Right

I could never do anything wright for my dad, everything was wrong, I loved him so much but I could never do any wright for him. I started school at 6, but I had some problems with my Health, I messed in my pants & the kids pushed me around & beat me up, I grow out of this at age 8, they put me in Spiecal Ed classes. I used to wait untill the bell would rang before I would go into class because I was ~~afr~~ ashamed to let people see me go in the class. I had a very hard time making friends, it seemed that people that had good & Healthy lifes, they wouldn't accept me because of my problems. All the people that I did Drugs & drank would accept me. At 11 I started smoking weed, all my uncles smoked, I would steal it from them out of there bedrooms + cars, they left it laying around so I took it. I went 12 years to school, after I got out of school I Met some people that did crystal, so I started snorfing it at age 18, when I was 22 this man moved to my town + he got me shooting it, then cocaine came along. I been married since I been 28 and quiet it all, I Kept beer in my house that set there about months at a time. I started having having problems with my marriage, my wife has depression problem that steemed from her being raped by her Dad, I didn't relized that the problem we had came from her being

raped by her Dad. It
was our annaviesory, I
cooked some steaks with
candle light dinner, I asked
my mother to keep the kids,
my wife didn't stay instead
she went to got the kids
and brought them back to
the House. My Brithday came
around + we both worked at
the same place, we were going
to take off work to go eat
+ have a good time but she
went to work, so I took off
and left. So I was riding
down the road + this man
flaged me down + I stoped
to see what he wanted, he
was sealing crack + I ended
up buying some from him. I
started taken money that was
for the bills to buy crack,
stecling money from my mother
to buy cracked. It started hurting
me, the things I was doing, I
would screm at God asking

him why my life had
ended up like this, I started
listening to the Bible tapes in
my car praying that my life
would get better, going to
church on wednesday & Sunday
still smoking crack. So I
went to my preacher and
told him what was going
on, he told me that his
Grand daughter went to the Haven,
I was baptized & saved
& then he ~~sne~~ sent me here.
Know me & my wife has a
better marrige then it ~~was~~
ever been, I am dedacated
to the program, I quiet
smoking the 2nd day I was
here, I never fealt better
~~the~~ about my life then I
do know. Jesus Christ is my
savior & I thank him for
my life today.
                    Thank you.

I Couldn't Save My Mama

tell ~ pg 83

My name is ████████ and this
is my testamoniey. when I was a young child
I was saved and excepted Jesus Christ in
my heart as my lord and saveur, but over
the past several year's i've been through
many triel's and tribulation's that led me in
to the dark and with that said I had turned
from a happy and hopeful young boy into
a lost and troubled young man who has been
runing from my past for some time. I beleave
I started goin a stray after my perent's
got a devorce when I was 11 and I
turned to smokeing weed are drinking!
Through my early year's as a young teen
I had my up's and down's with drug's
selling and useing, by the time I was
██ I thought I had gottin a grip on
my life and turned thing's around but
just when I thought I was doing good
my life was changed forever. Five day's befor
my B'day my mother committed suicied I
was there and wasn't able to prevent it from
happening or save her. I blamed myself for it...
So them after her death I started a long
four and a half year's of hard core drug
addiction involving oxy cotten, extacy, drinking,
crystal meth... Pretty much falling in what
I call "the gotta have it" stage of addiction
if it was there I didn't care I'd use it,
and that's not something I'm proud of.
I should have died many time's and because

I didnt end up in prision I new God was still there and would always be. In the last year the worst of the past Ten I went to jail six times, again Im not proud of this at all but I know if that had not happened I would have not opened my eyes and asked god to guid me back to the light, So Im here to say Im thankfull for being alive today without him I wouldnt be. It's taken me money months of praying and opening my heart to him to guide me here to the hell fighter's mission to mike shelly a man I've known and looked up too my whole life. Through god and this mission I beleave I'll find my place in life and no longer be lost but have peace and love in my life.

I Dated My Baby's Daddy

In ████, I lost a baby
that was premature, so I turned
to alcohol to hide my feelings
In ████, I started dating my
babies dad, And in ████,
he was in a real bad Accident,
when he recovered from that
he turned to drugs & alcohol.
In ████, I Started waitressing
in An adult Entertainment Club.
I worked there and started
dancing, Around the middle
of ████, I met this guy that
Eventually was my husband.
He started Abusing me,
mentally and physically. I
turned to drugs & alcohol
In ████, I found out I was
pregnant, so I quite my
job And my addiction.
In August ████, I had
my baby girl which is now
4 years old. In Sept. ████, me
And her dad got married

I started using again. I
got pregnant again in 2003,
but I couldn't stop my
addiction. I used all the
way up until I went into
labor. Thank god, that
he was a healthy little
boy. He will be 3 in
December 2006.
    In 2004, my dad
commited suicide, and I
found him dead in my
garage. The pain & hurt
was so bad, that I
started smoking dope,
shooting dope everyday.
    Me, my mom, and my kids
moved to a hotel. I met
this guy @ the hotel and
we started dating, I found
out I was pregnant. the
first part of my pregnancy
was hard to quite my
addiction.
    Me & my babe fiance

moved from ▓▓▓▓ to
▓▓▓▓▓▓▓ in January ▓▓▓
I gave birth to a precious
baby ▓▓▓ that passed
away of SIDS in June ▓▓▓▓▓
while in foster care.
     I ended up at the
▓▓▓▓▓▓▓ because July
▓▓▓▓, the judge gave
me my 2 children back
and a week later, I relapsed,
got drug tested, failed the
test, 3 wks later, they were
back in state's custody.
     I came here for Help
and I Graduate December ▓▓▓▓
     I Am glad I am here cause
now, I ~~can't~~ can take time
out for me + God.
                    Rhonda

RH's Note: In time Rhonda
will realize that time alone
won't fix anything. But time
with Jesus will. He is the
ultimate Healer and Restorer
of ALL THINGS GOOD!

I Decided To Become a Guinea Pig

"As a child growing up, I despised smoking and drinking alcohol. But when my parents got a divorce at age 14, everything changed. I have always had a fascination with how the mind works and how certain things effect it. So, I decided to be a guinea pig and experiment with drugs. And with my father out of the house, it gave me an opportunity to take action on my curiosity. At the age of 14, I smoked pot for the first time and it was absolutly amazing. All through high school I smoked it before school, during lunch break, and after school. I guess in some way I was trying to prove that you could use drugs and still maintain your life; I never skipped school, I only made 3 c's on my report card in my entire school career, I graduated with Honors and an advanced diploma. But pot wasn't enough, I began, at age 15, to buy other drugs to see how they would effect the mind. Cocaine, Acid, ecstasy, crack were all tried before I turned 16. I especially liked ecstasy, it made the world and everyone in it beautiful. I graduated High School at age 17, just when the "rave" scene in my hometown was exploding. So XTC became the Drug of choice for a couple of years until I found xanax. While attending college, I was diagnosed with General Anxiety Disorder, probably from the 500 or so X pills I had taken, was prescribed xanax. Never giving up pot, the two became essential during my college years. Eventually, I decided to give college a break and face the world on my own, moved in with a friend, started a landscaping business; sold cocaine, smoked crack without him knowing until finally I couldn't hide it anymore. I was the first time I went to rehab, it obviously did no good. I continued to sell coke, because I didn't have a job and had grown fond of not working and hanging out drinking all night, plus all the attention I was getting from the dealing, fed my ego. Well, soon my dope connection finally got busted and my business was over. I decided to move, only to discover a new way to get high, needles. The sudden rush from shooting a k-4 dilaudid was amazing. Within a couple of months I went from shooting one pill a day to 9 or 10. But when the cost of the pills went up from $10 to $25 it was cheaper to get a bag of heroin. So, luckily, this phase only lasted around 8 months until I got "dope sick" for the first couple of times. I had the world given to me and I denied it; paid college tuition, anything I needed or wanted. I thought I could do it on my own. So after an overdo on heroin and two overdoses on Xanax's I finally know there is a God. I could've just as easily passed out on my back instead of stomach and choked on the vomit! I thank my friend and ~~the Lord for getting me here. And~~ for my family FOR not giving up on me because I don't think I could've done it if the tables were turned So, with God's grace, I hope to finish school and start my career in medicine as I had planned since I was young; and to mainly stay clean to accomplish these goals.

I Did Not Want to Face the Truth

My name is ▮▮▮▮▮▮▮▮▮. This is my testimony. I was 7 yrs old and my cousin turned me on to beer and pot. He was 16 yrs old He gave me attention I didnt get from my dad. My dad was mean. as time went on he turned me on to pornography From there he molested ed me. I really didnt understand what was going on. So my using got stronger mean while at home my step-dad was hateful to me sometimes he would kick me in the but with boots on my feet would all most come off the ground. So I would Stay gone. By then I was adicted. I Started doing harder drugs opiates, benzo's, co-cane, LSD, getting introuble with school was every day when I went so I only went to get drugs or see girls Then leave. All I wanted to do was party. to keep my mind off Stuff I didnt understand or didnt want to Face. One day I came home after being gone For weeks. My mom and dad were Fighting. My dad called me into the room and said I'm not your real dad I don't know who your real dad is. you have to ask your mother. He was trying to hurt us both. I told him Im glad I don't care I don't like you any way. Im alive thats all that matters to me. So now I know why he was so mean to me. He was mad at mom 'For messing around on him. I have 3 Older sisters and a yonger brother. I felt better Knowing why he was mean to me. By Then I was shooting up coke, morphine, herion meth. anything I could Find. I was a Junkie in Full addiction. I went to rehab after rehab. That didn't work. I went through relationship after relationship untill I had my son I slowed down but didnt stop. She got tired of me going to jail barely making it. I had a good job For 17 yrs. but my addiction took every thing My Family house, car, truck, job, I was really lost then depressed, hurt, I wanted to die. which I have OD before but didit die. I have been in mental hospital's for being bypolar manic depression This last time I went for a nervous breck down. when I woke up IKnew where I was at but I couldn't talk good or see good. everything was blurry I. dont know how long I was there but after a while a nurse came up to me and said you are going to be discharge in a Few days you need can go home but you need help you need to look at this pamplet and Find a place you think might help you It had 2 pages of rehab's. all I could see was a smudged pace of paper →

Then I keep hooking and I Could make out warrior center out of all those places that is the only one I could read. SO I knew That the LORD was telling me to go there I had somebody to help me call I talk to Landon and he said come on I joined a 1 year deciple program. ▓▓▓▓▓▓▓▓▓▓▓▓▓ I know god wanted me there. I got saved before I came I knew I had to make a change. Then in the program I got baptized. I was a drug addict For 33 yrs now I live to help others in ▓▓ their addiction. I have been clean For 9 monts that Feels good. now me and my Stepdad are close he is the only dad I know. my mom is proud of me my hole Family is helping me get back to my Feet GOD is so good I am now 41 yrs Old and ready to live a good life. with my son and grandaughter. That is what life is worth living For. I want to Thank warrior center, The heart center and most of all GOD For giving me the ▓▓▓▓▓▓ chance to change and show love to others.

Hello Hellfighters,   Satan Sucks

My name is ████████████, I'm from
███████, La originally, but reside in Houma, La
for the last 20yrs. If you don't mind I would
like to tell you about myself.

I'm a full fledged cajun and I'm
grateful for my heritage. I am addicted to;
crawfish, shrimp, crabs, fish as well as a
few other things, such as; cocaine, weed, crystal meth,
pills, alcohol, and sex.

My introduction to alcohol and pot was around
the age of 12yrs. old and of course I didn't
have a problem, nor would it lead to other abuse.
Can you believe that I actually believed that
garbage? I now realize that I'm not as
intelligent as I gave myself credit for. I
graduated to cocaine by the age of 20 and all
other drugs soon followed.

I didn't consider myself an addict because, the
drugs & drinking didn't interfer with my job. I
continueally grew as a professional, I started as
an unexperience industrial radiographer assistant
at 19yrs of age to being the General Manager of
two companies by the age of 33yrs old. (NOT ALL BLESSINGS
ARE FROM God) I thought because I was successful
from a worldly stand point that my drugs &

drinking were under control. The whole time I
was neglecting my kids from there father, Even when
I was there, I wasn't there.

Then one day my friend, "Yea Right," introduced
me to crack and that really started my
demise. It grabbed a hold of me like nothing
has ever before. I would stay up all night,
knowing I had work the next morning, meetings,
whatever, it didn't matter I would just re-up to
get threw the day. I spent all my money on
it and when my money ran out I would pawn
things My bills weren't a factor, I just wouldn't
pay them. How smart is that? Nothing mattered to me
other than getting high. Keep in mind, I am the same
man that said, I don't have a problem.

There is a light at the end of the tunnel, however.
That light is called Jesus Christ. Who is my lord
& savior. He has changed my life forever.

I've shared some negative things about myself,
now I would like to share some positive things that
are happening to me, since I have accept Jesus'
as my Lord & Savior.

The first thing that I have noticed is
that he has delivered me from drugs, alcohol,
and tabaco. I mean delivered, no cravings,
no desire, no nothing. He allowed me

to come to his recovery center with a month of sobriety under my belt, so I could totally concentrate on the Lord. Which is a blessing in itself. Since my arrival here at this wonderful recovery facility the good Lord has also delivered me from diabetes! My blood sugar levels without medication is all the proof I need to say that to you, with this big smile on my face. If you think that is something, what about a piece of mind? How much is that worth? For me it's priceless!!!!

Thank you Jesus.

That's just a little bit of my testimony. I could go on forever about what God has done for me and how he has changed my life. There isn't enough paper in this book for that.

It would be an honor for me if you would accept this testimony as a fraction of my obligation of my Bearing the Standard For Our Lord Jesus Christ and allow me to be part of the HELLFIGHTERS.

I understand that you will be sending me a bible and a shirt. I am a XL and looking forward to wearing the Hell fighters colors. If at all possible a Satan Sucks tee shirt would be nice as well.

Your time and attention is greatly appreciated and as far as I can tell everyone on Campus looks forward to seeing and hearing from you

96

guys. Keep spreading the Love and glorifing Jesus.

From the heart of the Lords humble servant

"Blessed"

"And we know that all things work together for good to those who love God, to those who are the called according to His purpose."
Romans: 8.28

I Don't Remember Much

My name is ▮▮▮▮ and I am 28 years old. I grew up in ▮▮▮▮. I have a 2 yr. old daughter named ▮, and she is truly a blessing from God. I remember going to Church with my Grandmother when I was younger and it was a catholic church. I was baptized a young baby catholic. My Grandfather died when I was about 10 yrs. old and we moved so I began to go to Church of God with a friend who lived across the street. That con't for about a year. At age 13 I started using pot and drinking alchol. at age 16 I started using cocaine. My Mother is a alcholic and my Father a recovering alcholic of 17yrs. I didn't know my father until I was 18. my dad who adopted me and my mom got a divorce when I was 16 and that was where I really fell off the wagon. I cont. to use cocaine, putting all the hurt deep down and I also used other drugs to cover the pain. I overdosed at age 18. I don't remember much from age 18 until age 26 but at age 26 I got pregnant and was still really heavy on cocaine. I was by now using it to run from that. I was in my bed one night when I prayed to God to PLEASE let my baby be OK. I con't to pray but I still used. In fact I used until 2 weeks before I had my baby. I remember crying alot at nights just begging God to please help me and it was time to have my baby. Well, she didnt breath for 4 min after I had her and I had been praying the whole time I was in labor and calling on God. Its like the whole world stopped as she didnt breath. I then said whats wrong, is something wrong and God put the very breath of life in my little girl. as she began to cry I knew My God had heard my prayers and He answered them.

and so after this I got into pain pills, oxycottin and morphine. I got caught with cocaine and morphine back to back in like a 2 week period. I went to jail for 3 weeks and while I was in there I received my real very first bible on my 28th Birthday. I began to read it and was truly ready for a life change. I began to think back to my life and realized all the time I had ran with the devil and God was always there. I kept my faith and I was released on probation. Knowing I couldn't do it alone I wanted help and came to his Recover dr. T this and God has changed me and my life so much. I got saved and decided to know more about Jesus on ███ 16 '08. I know He has Great plans for me and I'm sure of it. My little girl is Healthy and its by the Grace of God. I could tell you now that I Know the right way is with God and I plan to give him way more then I gave the devil. I believe In God and know it is the only way.

Romans 7:25

I thank God through Jesus Christ our Lord. So then with the mind I myself serve the law of God; but with the flesh the law of sin

Med.

I Fell, But Got Up

Dear ███████████

My Name is ████████████ and I'm

Currently In a recovery center beening restored of what Satin has robbed me of. I was a back slidden Minister prior to comming here deep off in a life of drugs & fornication. While out there I ran into three other brothers in the same boat I was in, whom had fallen out of the ministry. I realized Just how brutal of a attack Satin has launched on God's Chosen Ones.

Actually I wanted to give up but my soul wouldn't let me.

See I was the Only One of the other four who had been actually on the streets ministering to the same ones I was now using drugs with. After having once been used to feed, shelter and even give the shoes of my feet & coat of my back I could see the disapointment in these brothers & sisters when they saw me back on drugs.

I'm so glad that "the Gifts and the calling of God are without repentence", Because God used a Conflict Satin was trying to use on my Job to finish me off to get me here to the place to restore me once again into that wonderful relationship I once had with my savior & Lord, Jesus Christ! Christ has even taken this experience to teach me the consequences of Compromise and given me the tools, & knowledge through the Holy Spirit to Once again to Live Victorious

Thanks, Yours In Christ

BACKSLIDING

O LORD,

When the world's unbelievers reject thee,

    and are so forsaken by thee that thou callest them no more,

    it is to thine own thou dost turn,

    for in such seasons of general apostasy

        they in some measure backslide with the world. *Rm. 12:1,2*

O how free is thy grace *Heb. 8:12, Micah 7.19*

    that reminds them of the danger that confronts them

    and urges them to persevere in adherence to thyself! *Rev 21:7*

I bless thee that those who turn aside

Lu. 15: 20-24   may return to thee immediately,

    and be welcomed without anything to commend them,

    notwithstanding all their former backslidings.

I confess that this is suited to my case, for of late

    I have found great want,

        and lack of apprehension of divine grace;

    I have been greatly distressed of soul

Is. 44:3 Jn. 7: 37, 38   because I did not suitably come to the fountain

    that purges away all sin;

    I have laboured too much for spiritual life,

    peace of conscience, progressive holiness,

    in my own strength. *Jn. 15:15*

I beg thee, show me the arm of all might;

Give me to believe

    that thou canst do for me more than I ask or think, *Eph. 3:20*

Heb. 13:5,6 → and that, though I backslide, thy love will never let me go,

    but will draw me back to thee with everlasting cords; *Jer. 31:3*

Is 43:2 ← that thou dost provide grace in the wilderness,

    and canst bring me out, leaning on the arm of my beloved; *Eph. 4:13*

    that thou canst cause me to walk with him

    by the rivers of waters in a straight way, *Ps. 23*

    wherein I shall not stumble.

Keep me solemn, devout, faithful, resting on free grace

    for assistance, acceptance, and peace of conscience. *Is. 26:3*

[86]

Write me anytime, BROTHER
Love in Christ,
Robert A. Smith
Matt 6:1-4
Jn 41:58:0
:)

Dear

As the son of, brother of, nephew of, and cousin of preachers, left out grandson of, I know what you are going thru, Been There, Done That! I lived for satan for 42 years, went to the HOG in '98, got truly saved in '99 and GOD reached down UNDER the miry clay, lifted me out, saved me from my father satan, from all the heinous, perverted life I existed in, adopted me & I became a Child of the KING, Hallelu}AH! I'm now a 51 year young minister for my Lord. HE's there for you my friend. EZ. 48:35.

I Finally Said NO!

The Testimony

I have been Addicted to pain meds and alcohol for 12 years. At the age of 15 I took my first Pain pill, Loctab, At the age 13 I took my first Xanx. When I got into High School, I started drinking real bad. My dad used to give me pain meds and Alcohol all the time. I did Finish High School, but still doing drugs, such as, smoking marijuana, pain meds. and Alcohol. I quit For a year due to an over dose of Acid and cocaine I became Non-socialibly, I was like in a Coccoon. I staid at my grandmothers house and Never came out, for a year. I Finally did Something about it, I joined the National Guard and became a solider. Well, while I was in the Guard I picked drinking and pain meds back up, Im about 24 now. When I got out of the guard, I went to school to become a Casino dealer. Right back into the situation I was in High School. Had a house, fine car, lost everything do to Alcohol and drugs. Well, I Always had the Lord in my life, but I put alcohol + drugs First. I got stabbed in the neck by my own brother and almost dieded, I was still using drugs. After 7 years of drinking and drugging, I Finally want to put the Lord First. I enrolled

At this Recover Center back in
July. The Lord talked to me back
in July. They was a bunch of guys
making alcohol and ofcourse, I wanted
in on it. That Day in class and Ephesians
5:17-18 hit me in the face, I turned right to
it. It says Therefore do not be unwise., but understand
what the will of the Lord is. And do not be
drunk with wine, in which is dissipation; but
be filled with the Holy Spirit. I thought about
for awhile, but still wanted to drink with
those guys. Later that night, I went to Chapel
and opened the door for the preacher from
Gulfport, we talked. He asked me to give a
testimony of why I was here, I got scared
but didn't refuse him. I prayed to God
to give me strentgh and understanding to
face my fears of being infront of a
audience. I gave my testimony in 10 min. and
got a standing ovation, it felt wonderful.
That night we played football. Now, we was
suspose to drink this night. I got hurt,
caught a knee to the face, had to end up
having surgery under my eye. After I got
hurt I came in my room and laid
down. Those guys still came to my room
and asked me to drink, I told them,
NO, ya'll can have it. The next day I
went to the doctor and those guys got
kicked out. Now, I'm back at the
after doing 5 wks, I have to start over.
which is o.k. I not here for time, I'm here

For myself. Ima doing great Now, my
vision is still a little off, but I'm happy
I'm back. God sent me back here to
get the full effect of this program.
I'm in week 0 Now, but still in my
studies and understanding the Lord
a lot better. This is the testimony
of a 32 year old young man thats finally seeing
the Light.

Sincerely

I Got Sick and Tired of
Being Sick and Tired

Dear Mr. Koe

Hello, my name is ███████████, I wanted
to write and share my testimony with you. I'm
a recovering crack attic. I started smoking
it about 4 years ago. Growing up I was
always into sports and all kind of outdoor
activities I enjoyed it. I had a great
family And Never got into trouble with the law
Never did drugs but I did start drinking
when I was about 16 when I turned 17
I tried my first Joint Didn't really care for
it. I quit school earlie and mess up a few
Scholarships I could had gotten playing
Baseball. By the time I turned 21. I got
in trouble with the law for Burgly. I got
5 years probation, ~~Finding~~ & Ended up messing
that up and went to the pen. After about a
year in there. I started smoking Ciggaretts.
and trying weed. when I got out I still
smoked weed. Then started trying more stuff
Like Cocain, Meth, that went on for years
then one day a friend of mine wanted
me to try ~~to~~ some Crack with him and I
did. It was one of the worse mistakes of
my life. I Lost just about every thing I
had. I Got where I was Stealing from
my family or who ~~ever~~ ever just to

get high. Then I got into trouble again
I should be dead. but I always knew
that God was looking out for me. But I was
running from him. I got locked up again and
done a year and now I'm back on probation.
Then I got into trouble since. ~~(crossed out)~~
I have 2 kids. my little boy is 5 and my
little girl is 2. I have both of them. But
God started talking to me and I was sick
and tired of benging sick and tired. I was
sick of living the way I was. It broke
my heart when me and my kids would ride
by a store and my son would asked to stop
and buy him some gum and all I had on
my mine was a piece of Rock. So I got
down on my knees for 3 nights in a row
and asked the lord for help. And I got sent
here to this recovery center. I couldn't ask
for a better blessing. I've been here for a month
and a half. And God has really blessed me in
so many ways. I'm very thankful that Jesus
layed down his life for me and the world.
I feel so free and I'm not sick of being
sick and tired anymore. Jesus freed me
from my bondage. And I'm thankful for
that. I plan on serving him whole heartly
for the rest of my days.

I want to be a WARRIOR for the LORD.
My UNClE ███████ use to say before
He died (Ain't God Good.) He is wonderful
And ⊘ Again I thank him for what he
hAs done for me and what he's gonna do.
For me IN My life. Thank you for taking
up the time to read this. MAy God Bless
You And I'll Keep you In My prayers

God Bless

God is Awesome!

I Had Never Known
Happiness Without Drugs

My name is ███████████ I'm 35, and I have 3 beautiful children. I started drinking and using drugs at the age of 13. My dad was an alcoholic, and he taught me to mix drinks for him, so I would steal rum from him and drink it. I had a rare bone disorder they (doctors) discovered when I was 13. My bone in my foot died, and was replaced with my hip bone and fused in   The surgery was unsuccessful, and I have lived with chronic pain since it was discovered. That's when I became addicted to painkillers. I used any and every drug I could find to escape from the harsh and painful reality of my life. I struggled with depression all my life as well. I never knew happiness without drugs and alcohol. It gave me the feeling I had been looking for all my life. I was put in treatment for drugs and alcohol when I was 16, I stayed clean for 3 years, until I relapsed in college. I used continuously until I came to this recovery center in July. My mom is a born again Christian (as of 1988). She searched for many many years for God. She has been my spiritual role model for years. In December   I lost my sons to my x-husband when I was arrested. After that, I felt like my life was over. I simply had no will to live. I attempted suicide twice. It is a miracle I am alive today! Since I have been here at Rehab I have rededicated my life to Jesus Christ. The hardest thing for me is to surrender my past - the hurts and pain I caused my children and family - and completely rely and trust in Him for my future. But what a relief it is to know that God can do anything! That He wants me not to just be truly happy, but joyous (in good times and adversity) and TRULY FREE! I know a freedom and a soul-felt joy I have NEVER known! I believe He has completely delivered me from addiction and depression. Now I am working on claiming His promise for deliverance from cigarettes. That's a hard one not to take back several times a day. But God is faithful! He finishes what He starts, and what a mighty work He has started in me! As we like to say here, "My God is in the HEALING BUSINESS!"

I hope I have explained my testimony in enough detail - I could write 20 more pages!

Thank you for what you do - it is much appreciated!

I Had Six Step Dads

My name is ▊▊▊▊▊▊▊, a good Friend gave me a pamplet "Son of A Preacher Man" And Said if I give my and testimony I would recive Something. Well I would be more than Happy to Speak on How god Saved a wretch like me.

▊▊▊▊▊▊▊▊▊▊▊▊▊▊▊▊ Im 24 yrs. old. growing up for me was fairly comfortable. My monther was a college grad and was persident of South▊▊ Bank. My ▊DAD▊ owned his own ▊▊▊▊ business. We lived in ▊▊▊▊ GA until I was 3 yrs old, They divorced and my mother gained custody from then on, she was divorced + remerried Six times. that was a struggle on its own my Dad never gave up He always came and pick me up on weekends and holidays. I can always rember He would say John dont call me your Father because our Father is in heaven + He always said the lords prayer to me at night. I guess living with six differint stepdads was hard because I learned alot about things that your not supposed to do By the age 7 I was smoking cigerrtes + Drinking beer but I never told my dad. By the age 14, I was selling priscripton drugs + weed For my last stepdad ▊▊▊, ▊▊▊, I was taking advantage of underage girls that were my age. At the Age of 22, I did my First Bid in prison, thinking How cool was it going to be when I get out

And could tell all my Friends. Well I met.
One of the most influential persons In my
life who I now have a 1 yr old with and
Im married to. She decided When I got out
of prison that Her and my Dad would Have
a long talk with me about seeking help in
a rehab, Well I thought about it and said
What for? I dont have a problem! that very
next Week my parole officer, gave me a
drug test and then gave me an option back
to prison or rehab. Now I know that the
probation officer had nothing to do with it
but it was by grace + mercy of my lord
and Saviour. Well Im now at the mission
of Hope on a 90 day program Wich have
givven a chance to take a closer walk with
my god and I have become saved and
my realationship with my dad is great Im
Seeing life in a whole new light. I
Just want to say,

Thank you jesus for saving me.

God Loves \
Jesus Saves / Amen

I Have a Big Problem

Dear Friends with Hell Fighters —
 Hello. My name is ▓▓▓▓▓ & I
am currently at the ▓▓▓▓▓▓
Haven for Women in ▓▓▓▓▓▓. I
am a devout christian who has
been saved since I was 14 years old.
But, recently in my life, I've been
faced with obstacles that led me
to make some really bad choices. I am
a registered nurse and have been
for 5 years. I've practiced in the
hospital setting & in the office setting
more recently. I have a 14 month
old son & a wonderful husband who
both love me very much. But, Lord —
How BADLY I'VE HURT THEM! Over
the past 6 months, I've struggled
with prescription drug abuse. Most of
the time, the medication was prescribed
to me & I took it only as directed.
But, when life seemed to get hard
(with finances, being a mom, being a
wife) I would abuse my medication.
And, if I didn't have any more of my
pills left, I would steal them....
FROM MY OWN MOTHER. Eventually
my problem got worse & my family
could tell a difference in my demeanor.
I would have slurred speech, drooping
eyes, & would be very forgetful &
sleepy. The medication caused me to
become impulsive.... I would SHOPLIFT
while having a purse full of money.

Then, the day after I shoplifted, I would become sober & wonder where I got it... I would have absolutely NO RECOLLECTION of the day before! My husband began to question my behavior & ask me if I was "on something". I would tell him that I was "just fine & I'm just tired & stressed out, Don't worry." Then, my husband began to investigate. When he began to doubt me... He found out all of the TRUTH. He found out that I shoplifted... He knew the owner's of the boutique from which I shoplifted — & they told him that they caught me shoplifting. And the worst part of all, "MY son WAS WITH ME & I WAS "HIGH" & shoplifting! Then I began to allow my addiction to affect my career. As a nurse, I have the credentials that qualify me to call in medications. Well I successfully called in my own medication. My husband found out about this as well. I only did it once, BUT ONCE WAS ENOUGH. That's when I realized, "████ — YOU HAVE A PROBLEM!". I confessed to the pharmacist what I'd done & I did not take the medication. I called the Mississippi Board of Nursing & turned myself in. I was absolutely horrified & embarrassed. All I could think about was God. How dissapointed he must be!? My wonderful husband designed an intervention. He secretly gathered my closest family members & called a meeting. This meeting was a HUGE SURPRISE to me. My addiction was a secret... MY SECRET. Now, everybody knows! How humiliating!? But now, I realize that my husband helped to "set me free". That very night, I got "REAL WITH GOD." It became evident to me that God was also at that meeting on that night. He led me to the ▓▓▓▓▓▓ and here, I know with all of my heart, that this was a divine appointment with God. And I'm not here by mistake — Because God doesn't make mistakes. I've lost alot of things over the past 6 months — But God has given me a chance to redeem myself & make it right. I trust my Father, I am going to take his hand & walk with him. I will close with scripture... my very favorite: "And ye shall know the truth and the truth shall make you free." —John 8:32!

Love,
▓▓▓▓▓▓

I Just Wanted to Fit In

My name is ████████ and I am an alcoholic. I would to share with you my story.

I had a wonderful childhood. There was no abuse, actually I may have been spoiled with material things. Although my spiritual life was not up to par, I was baptized at the age of twelve. I really should say I was dunked in water. I went to church because my parents told me to and I was baptized because I was told I needed to be. Although there was a belief in God and a temporary spiritual feeling, I know now there should have been a lot more.

As a teenager I never caused any problems. My grades show that I didn't apply myself and I was probably not the sharpest tack in the box either. I don't mean I failed anything but I didn't make All A's either.

When I went to college ████████ I was introduced to pot and I liked the feeling. Besides, all my friends did it and I wanted to fit in with the crowd. I only finished or I should say almost finished 2 years before I got a really good summer job. When fall came I stayed with my job and didn't go back

to school. I moved out of my parents
house, bought a fast boat and just had
a great time. I continued to smoke pot
and drank very little.

At the age of 25 I got married to
a wonderful young lady. We smoked pot on
a regular basis at night after work.
Still I was not a big drinker. It was
more social than anything. We had our
first child when I was almost 29. My
wife never smoked pot while she was
pregnant and I slowed down during this
time. After the baby we started
smoking again. When our child was about
3 years old we quit cold turkey. We
really wanted to be good parents. We had
another girl in 19██ and we were a happy
little family. We did dance recitals and
church every Sunday. The girls grew up
in Sunday school. It was great.

At first I began to have a drink at
night. Whiskey and 7up was my drink.
At first it was 1 each night and as time
and the pressures of a new business
it went to 2 and then 3 or 4. What
ever it took to be able to sleep. Through
this we still went to church on Sundays.

But I got nothing out it. We moved to
Clarksdale, Ms in ███ and I hated it.
It is where my wife's family lived. It ended
up being a blessing for my children because
of the drugs in Moss Point.

My wife divorced me in ███ and rightfully
so. Alcohol was controling my life. After my
divorce I drank even more. I lived alone
out in the country and loneliness was my
enemy. I quit drinking for about 9 months
after my youngest girl had me picked
up and evaluated. They didn't put me
in rehab that time but the next time
I voleeteerd to go. I did a 28 day
12 step that left God out and it
was worthless. I lost my resturant while in rehab.

I moved back to the coast as soon
as I got out and moved in with my sister
and her family. They do NOT allow any drinking.
So I would sneak around but I got caught
after about a year and they kicked
me out. I managed to keep my job
throughout, some how.

I lived in a tent and drank for 2
weeks and finally decided that I've
had enough and came to this recovery place
I have recieved the Lord, surrendered

my life and got baptized. I have
learned more about Jesus since I've
been here than I had in 53 1/2 years.
My new life is great and I am really
looking forward to carrying my cross
for Jesus. I know he will let me know
when I'm ready and which cross to carry
and when to start. I'm preparing for
the journey.
    I look foward to the day I see
Jesus but I know he has some things
for me to do here first.
    Thanks for listening and God Bless You.
            In Love with Jesus

I Kept Trying

My name is ███████████████
I was born in Fort Lauderdale Florida
████████████ My parents name are
████████████ and ███████████████. I have
a sister name ████████████████. My
parents got divorced when I was 10 years
Old so me and my sister stay ████ with
my mother. During that time of my mom
getting divorce she went to a tent meeting
that Pastor ████████ had and she got
saved in around ████ As a child I
grew up going to church 2 times a
week. I went through School - When
I became a teenager at the age of 16
I smoke my first joint in my 12 grade
year but it was not a problem at that time.
I graduated from High school and start
working. I did not go to college because my
mom did not have the money. Doing my
younger age about 13 year of ago I got saved
████ During a revival in Fort Lauderdale
From then God had a calling in my life.
I did not have girlfriend that much in my
life but I work in Security Guard work
For some year. I was reading my Bible

and going to church but throughout my
life I would go to Night club + stripper
bar OVER Fort Lauderdale, Florida I know
the Lord was speaking to me about being in
these places but I kept on doing it. In my
29 YEAR I decide that I want to move
Away From my mom to ████ GA. For
a New start oF life. I had Alway want
to drive a truck 18 wheeler. In ████
I apply to School oF Truck Driving in
Indiana So I went For 4 weeks I got
my CDL License and had I drive For
████ Transport For a Year contract and
around ████ I want to Fulfull my Fresh
desires oF Sex and was introduce to
crack cociane Smoking it through the Grass
pipe and From that my life has never
been the Same - From age oF 30 to 39
I had a struggle Smoking crack Cociane
I went to many Rehab. places but
Never been clean For Some time.
████████████████████
████████ I went to ████████
Rescue mission program graduate in ████
right After hurricane Irve came through
and WAS about 6 months Clean and I
fail again and Went back on + oFF

smoke crack cocaine. I meet a
man in a meeting for Most Excellent
way for Drugs and Alcoholics people his name
was ▓▓▓▓▓▓ that he became my
mentor I look up to and he has been
A blessing to me. Scott kept telling
me about a recovery center with a Christain
base program that can help me in
my defent from my addiction that
I came in here ▓▓▓▓▓▓▓▓ on
monday. My life have been changed
and my mind have been restored in
Jesus christ I did ask Jesus christ
to forgive me a coup or weeks
before I came to this recovery center
I have been deliver from my addictio
because I told the Lord I am going to
save him for the rest of my life. Jesus
has been to good to me. ▓▓▓▓▓▓▓
▓▓▓▓▓▓▓▓▓▓ I will graduated
on ▓▓▓▓▓▓▓▓▓▓ at 2:00 clock Friday.
I have a relationship with Jesus christ
my Lord. ▓▓▓▓▓ Please pray that
Jesus Christ will have his way in my
life and pray for the men + women
at this recovery center

Your Truly,

I Knew How To Make
All the Boys Happy

Dear friends,

I was always a good person. Kind hearted,
loved animals, tomb boy. Loved everyone
and everything, especially having fun.
I'd climb trees and ride on the handle
bars of bikes as a child for fun. As I
got older it was theme parks that I
enjoyed. I was fearless to some degree.
I loved an adventure!

I was born to teenage parents in Ann
Arbor, MI. Both my grandfathers worked
for Ford Motor Co. When I was 12 my
father's best friend molested me. He went
to jail for a little more than a year.
Upon his release, my mother was convinced
that it was the alcohol that caused him
to do this to me. So she reunited our
family. It happened again... this time
it was me who was sent away, to live
with his sister in Arkansas. I felt alone,
confused, and thrown away. But I still
wanted to go "home". I began high school
and drinking, going to parties at the lake.
Boys seemed to really like me and since
I knew how to make them happy, well
I did. At least I felt loved.

At the age of 17 I was pregnant.
My aunt sent me to Florida to live
with my grandmother because she couldn't
deal with a baby and of course my
mother didn't want me (her competition
as she saw it) to intrude on her sick
little marriage. (sorry, still working on forgiveness)

So I had a beautiful baby boy. My mother said my life was over. I enrolled into college and worked waitressing at night. College was fun, we drank, smoked pot. Went to the clubs in Gainesville, Fl and discovered extasy. WOW! Dancing all night, endless friends. But I was empty. I went to church a couple times with my friends and always wished my family was like "them." They all were so nice and loving and accepting. I met a man, he wasn't very religious, and fell out of the church habit.

We smoked pot regularly, for me it was to numb all my pain. We had alot of problems.

Two little girls later... things were getting worse. We seperated yet again. I thought money would make me happy. I began a career in sales and was very successful. I met a man whoms father was a neuro surgan and mother a nurse, sister was a lawyer. He introduced me to cocaine. I was so happy, having fun going on several vacations, the boats, the cars, the everything, was too good to be true. He asked me to marry him after 2 months, I said yes, (of course) Soon my nose was so messed up, he said well we can smoke it. I said "really?" Didn't know that. He grabbed a spoon, some baking soda, And that was the beginning of the end! <u>My hell quickly surrounded me.</u> He was such a loser and mood swings like Dr. Jekyl / Mr. Hyde. Proud, puffed up because of his <u>daddy's</u> money. I seen it for what it really was. I broke it off. But my addiction was there, tapping on my shoulder. "PSST, HEY!" "FEED ME!" I never experienced this feeling before but had remembered his "friends" number. They were happy to "<u>Help</u>". (ya right) They taught me, how too's. I didn't know it was CRACK, at first.

But it got bad, I lost my self respect, what was left of my self worth, my dream of being in a rich family, my kids (almost) my family hated it, they tried to stop it, couldn't. nothing helped, I was in the biggest stronghold ever! It haunted my dreams.

In May I came to the conclusion it was going to kill me. <u>The darkness was swallowing me up.</u> The pain I was causing created guilt and shame.

June 17th I came to this recovery center I found Lord God, my saver, I am a new Creation. I am a new **woman** and mother. I have a hope now for a fulfilled righteous future with the love of a wonderful new father. And the best part ... <u>I'm whole for the first time in my life.</u> I'm worth alot more than I did before because I've been forgiven. I <u>never</u> have to go back.

And I will never go back to the darkness.
Thank you Jesus, Restorer, Healer, Lover,
Father, Comforter, Creator.

I beleive all this happened for a
reason, and the reason is because He
loved me and wanted me near.

One day I will give back and work
for my church in the Most Excellent
Way ministry in PC, FL.

Thank You.

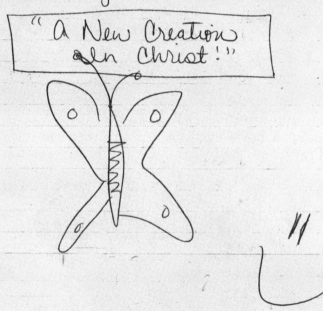

"A New Creation
In Christ!"

Hope
Love
Faith

I can't wait to begin my new life ☨

I Lost My Cherry When I Was 12

Dear Hellfighters:

My name is ███ I was raised with two older sisters and one younger sister and both parents. My mom took me and my sisters to church every Sunday, and even though I was saved around age 7, I didn't have a "relationship" with God. Being such a sensitive, tender-hearted child, my feelings were always being hurt about something. My dad loved me greatly, but he was very strict and he yelled a lot. When I was twelve I started experimenting with alcohol and lost my virginity. I continued "looking for love in all the wrong places" through alcohol, cigarettes, drugs, and promiscuity. When I was 16 I got pregnant, got married at 17, then divorced at 19. When I was 24 I met a man, we moved in together and were engaged, but I got pregnant before we got married. On my ███ birthday I had my second child by this same man. My oldest sister started going to a new church, became excited about God, and was living right with God. She had been inviting me to go to church every chance she got for about a year. I finally agreed to go and God's presence was noticeable the first time I walked through the doors. I struggled and fought God for a while, but God never gave up on me. He showed His love for me and started healing my heart. I was in love with God and life. I stopped drinking and doing drugs. I laid down things that would create a wall between God and me, like listening to secular music, and instead fell in love with worship music. I was living for God for about 3 years until I started compromising. I said, "It's okay to have just one drink," and "what will it hurt to take just one pill." Then "I'll just miss one Sunday, I really want to rest." "My bible-reading can wait until tomorrow." Things were a "slow fade" over the next two years. Then my dad was diagnosed with pancreatic cancer. This was in addition to my husband (yes, the father of my two children) being sick and out of work for 1½ years. My daddy died four months later and that when I lost it. I actually did things I would have sworn that I would never do. I realize now that God was there with me the whole time, watching over me, just <u>waiting for me to turn to him and mean it</u>, not just the passion of the moment. After two months of falling apart God led my family, who confronted me, and they brought me to the Home of Grace. Now God has taken a broken woman and made me whole again. I can have grief, but grief can't have me. God is my Father, He loves me, and He will take care of me. I am the prodigal daughter! I have been here 5 weeks and am so excited to see all of the miracles God is going to do during my next 8 weeks, then what He will do when I go home. God is teaching me and it is not always easy, but I'm giving all control to God this time. I have stopped smoking cigarettes for 11 days, and that is a miracle! Now the Lord is the spirit, and where the spirit of the Lord is there is freedom!

2 Corinthians 3:17

Thank You and Love in <u>Christ Jesus</u>,

I Love My Dad

Dear Hellfighters,

My name is ████████████. I'm currently incarcerated at ███████ County Adult Detention Center. I just finished reading your New Testament Hellfighters handbook. I loved it! I attended a Christian recovery center this summer. I graduated July 9th. That's where I first heard of ya'll. But I had to return here to await my court date and see where God will bring me next. There was a girl here that had your handbook so I recognized immediately and had to read it. After reading it, I realized how great it would be for my dad to have one of your handbooks. My dad's name is ████████████ He is incarcerated at the ██████████ Correctional Facility in ████████. He is 60 years old and has been riding motorcycles his whole life. At first I was so upset that he was going to jail at his age. But now I see just like with everything in life God has a plan. Because he is now reading the Bible and seeking the Lord. After all these years it is truly a blessing to know that my dad is going to find his way to God. But I can't help but think that reading your handbook and hearing the testimony of men like him would help him so much with the little struggles he still has with his faith. So I'm sending his address, and if you could find it in your heart to send him a copy I think it would really help him and mean the world to me. Thank you very much for your time and God bless you and all those who help you with your ministry.

Sincerely,

I Married My Babysitter

To: Hellfighters Staff,

Hi! Let me start by telling a little about myself. My name is ████████████ i'm 38 years old I live in ████████████ I had a good life. I was married at the age of 20 to my high school sweetheart. We had 3 children over a ██ year period. But I was never faithful to her and ended up getting devorice only to marry the girl who babysitted my kids. She was 19 and I was 31 we had a child. But again I just couldn't be a faithful husband. I left to go to the store oneday and to this day I never returned that was about 3 year ago.

During those 3 years I lost my job at ████████████ Offshore where I was a struc. welding General Foreman. After lossing my job I started cooking Meth on a daily basic. At first I was balling making up to $1,000°° a day had 4 or 5 cars, big screen T.V.s etc. Just living day by day. It got to where people would trade anything they had for my dope. They called it on the streets ████████████ because

I have a ████████ tatoo on my arm. Then one day I got busted of poss. of precur. chemails with intend to manuf. I stayed in jail of █ weeks with a $500,000°° bond that was March & ████ when I got out of jail my so called friends had stoled everything I owned. So I decided the only way to get back on my feet was to bust off one more bacth of meth and quit. But it didn't work out that way cause I was making more money than ever. And getting back on my feet. Trading dope for any and everything out there. I will never forget the day I traded 2½ grams of dope for a daimond ring a girl had. After she never return with the $175°° she owed me I took it and got it appraised and guy who appraised it offered me $5000°° for the stone. Man I thought to myself whats going on out there. But I was living high and stanting to get back on my feet. But then on ████ After ingoring ██ all the warning signs

I was getting. Such as several close calls
with the law. Allmost getting caught manuf.
but somehow I would always slip out the back
door and get away. Getting pulled over with
dope knowing if I got caught I wouldn't be
able to get out of jail. But I always had
this sixth sences. Its like I knew when to
cook and when to shut it down and get out of
there. But on this day when I woke up on
the morning of FeB.5 I knew I was going to
get in trouble. Even my girlfriend at the time
told me that morning to be careful that she
had a bad feeling. But I ingored the feeling
and did what I know I didn't need to do.
I had a pocket full of dope. But wanted to
cook a bacth so I would be ready for the
weekend. And sure as I know it at 7:00 o'clock
that evening I got pulled over in VANCLEAVE
And got another precursor charge. And was
booked at the ████████ in ████████ with no
chance of getting a bond. I was looking

At 68 years and a 2 million dollar fine.
My life was basicly over. I hired the best
lawyers in ████████. Which was ████████
and ████████. But still the best deal
they could get me was 15 years with 5 suspended
and 10 to do. I was scared to death not knowing
what to do. So I started reading my Bible and
praying only because I was scared and lost.

   And from out of the blue a public
defender I had talked when I first got to
jail came by just to check on me. By this
time she had started her own law firm. She
asked me if I would let her take over my
case free of charge. So I thought what can
I loss, so I fired my other lawyers and with
in a week she came to me with a sentence
of 7 years suspended with the completion of
the R.I.D. program in ████ country prison. Within
2 weeks I was in court. And within 30 day I was
at the ████ Not realizing that God didn't
want me in prison for 10 years I was planing

to get out of the ▓▓▓▓ in 5½ months
and getting back at it. So I got out of the RID
on ▓▓▓▓ and on ▓▓▓▓ I was back cooking
Meth. and balling not reporting to probation, just
running wild. Got in the best relationship in my life
with a girl I've known all my life. For the first
time in my 38 year I was in love. But I still had
a problem with being faithful to her, because of the
drugs and I lost her because of it. But on
▓▓▓▓ I got caught spotlighting deer and
caught a convicted felony with a firearm charge.
which is a mandentory 5 year sentens. But
again somehow by the grace of God my probation
officer and the Criminal Invest. Deptment at
the ▓▓▓▓ County Shaffal Deptment didn't
want to throw me away. And instead of
the 5 year they sent me here to this Christian
Rehab Center for 3 months. I've been here
for 2 month, I've become the Pres. of clients
I've rededicated my life to Jesus. And
I starting to relize how he works

in peoples life. And I know he's plan
for me wasn't to spend the rest of my
in jail he's got a bigger and ~~a~~ better
~~job~~ job for ~~my~~ me in the future. And being
~~a~~ I'm a ~~█████████~~ baseball coach. I
believe it got to be help the youth
in my local area come to Jesus Christ
as their Lord and Savior. Because my
life when I graduate from here on
~~██████~~ is not going to be drugs but to
help other with Gods Word.

I Needed Some Relief

To ▓▓▓▓▓▓▓▓▓▓▓▓▓▓▓▓▓▓

My name is ▓▓▓▓▓▓▓▓ I checked in this Rehab Center at the end of July. Drinking to much slacking at work, on the verge of a nearvous break down. I went to my boss ask for a monday or friday off so I could detox. And quit drinking. He informed me that I needed to find the lord and learn to live my left right. I ask how. He told me about ▓▓▓▓▓▓▓▓ said it was a two week program He's called ▓▓▓▓▓▓▓. They Faxed him an application I called ▓▓▓▓▓▓ he informed me it was a 90 day program. understand this is our busy season as im in construction. Also I worked for this man 20 some yrs. ago for 3 or 4 yrs when he was first starting any way he paid my fee + let me off work since i've been here. I can't see any diffrence but people here say it is tramatic. I know I don't cuse as much not at all actualy I pray a lot read the bible daily. And I hate to read but, I really enjoy the bible. I've been in and out of Church ▓▓▓▓▓ all my life. And 3 or 4 Rehabs but nothing like TH ▓▓▓▓▓▓▓▓▓▓▓▓. They are genuine ly interested and want to help people like me I'm the past I've been anxous to get out and start using this time w/ jesus in the empty void in my heart I'm going to make it now. Today was a great day Because I went to ocean springs to sign some paper work and could dietress

sea↑

in the ladys eyes ask her about it she was
kinda supprised told me a little. Out of
nowhere I ask if she went to church
this really stepped back so to speak
(kinda shocked) she said no but she prayed
all the time. I had heard that one before
Not that I've ever asked that Question
but that was my ~~answer~~ answer when
I was asked that Question. my story started
in '84 or '85 I had been audited by I.R.S. Didn't
Know, was married two step children. Not
mature enough for that much responcibilaty
anyway marriag. on rocks after only 10 mts
we weren't saved. From what I'm understanding
It was not a Godly marage as she was devorced
anyway IRS. started garnishing my wages
more stress, she devorced me I was tore up
Quit my job took off on the road with a
~~pho~~ telemarketing crew working for cash.
Talk about life in the fast lane. For a young
nieve country boy drugs shooting up.
Whores you name it (no Homo stuff)
settled down in califorina for a few yrs.
w/ Lady 14 yrs older. that ended ████ when
my mom died went Back to mo. where I
was orignally from. Got in church w/ my
aunt + uncle for a little ~~while~~ while. But
drugs + boose + ~~woo~~ women started again
Tryed ~~to~~ Rehabs no dice finally after
three attempts at suicide. One almost
worked went to rehab a godly woman
at stress center told me about a Hale way
House in Cuba   , It was a joke

I fell after only 4 mts was homeless
called the guy I now work for again
after 20 yrs he said he had work for me
not any I shoveled snow and got down
here mid December and here I am a much
happier man this last month month
but be four I got to rehab. but before
this I was miserable Thank the good
lord for sending me to this
wonderfull place. and giving me the
cani to get the program.

God Bless

Thank you all
I need the large print Bible
in the new King James

I Pulled the Plug on Mama

Hey Mr. Smith!

I just read your tract that someone was kind enough to give me here at the rehab center. I can relate to your story; as me myself, I am an addict. I've been using some 15 years off and on now. I ran full throttle into drugs for about 12 years with the last 3 yrs having spells of cleanness or sobriety. Those clean spells were always when I was going to church and living for the LORD. Seems like I would have realized that Christ delivers. After this last relapse, I told myself, I was going to the rescue mission to recieve GOD's grace, GOD willing.

I've lost a lot of people "literally" along the way. My mom "~~XXX~~" overdosed while I was partying with her about three years ago. I gave her oxygen or CPR, but after she was on lifesupport for a week we had to pull the plug on her. It hasn't been easy. I've lost two cousins in the past year 2 yrs. to drugs also. I was close to both of them, and I miss both of them. My mom drank everyday, and she was shaking by 8:00am without a drink. I have 5 generations of alcoholics in my bloodline, and that's just as far as we can count. I know, that I know, with the LOVE and GRACE of CHRIST he will deliver me. He's already doing it. I have a long way to go for him though.

Sincerely,

GOD BLESS

FEBRUARY 14

SOVEREIGN GRACE

Peace, Grace, and Glory

There is a great deal of difference between law and grace. "Being justified by faith we have peace with God through our Lord Jesus Christ; by whom also we have access by faith into this grace wherein we stand, and rejoice in hope of the glory of God." There are three precious things here: peace for the past; grace for the present; and glory for the future. There is no peace until we see the finished work of Jesus Christ—until we can look back and see the cross of Christ between us and our sins. When we see that Jesus was "the end of the law for righteousness," that He "tasted death for every man," that He "suffered, the just for the unjust," then comes *peace*. Then there is "the *grace* wherein we now stand." There is plenty of grace for us as we need it—day by day, and hour by hour.

Then there is *glory* for the time to come. A great many people seem to forget that the best is before us. Dr. Bonar says that everything before the true believer is "glorious." This thought took hold of my soul; and I began to look the matter up and see what I could find in Scripture that was glorious hereafter. I found that the kingdom we are going to inherit is glorious: our crown is to be a "crown of glory"; the city we are going to inhabit is the city of the glorified; the songs we are to sing are the songs of the glorified; we are to wear garments of "glory and beauty." Furthermore, our society will be the society of the glorified; our rest is to be "glorious"; the country to which we are going is to be full of "the glory of God and of the Lamb."

Many are always looking on the backward path and mourning over the troubles through which they have passed. They keep lugging up the cares and → *I Pt. 5:7* anxieties they have been called on to bear and are forever looking at them. Why should we go reeling and staggering under the burdens and cares of life when we have such prospects before us?

If there is nothing but glory beyond, our faces ought to shine brightly all the time.

D. L. MOODY

Write me anytime
Love in Christ
Robert L. Smith
Matt. 6:21
Ps. 147:3

Dear
We cannot
change or forget the past, but, we
can learn from it. Then, we look to the future,
put as much of God's Word, JESUS, in us and
then we have no time to think on the past. after
all, yesterday is a canceled check, today is cash
and tomorrow is a promissory note. Since God
made the Promise, II Cor. 1:20, 7:1, II Pt. 1:4, I Jn. 2:25,
I know, my past is filled with mud, blood & beer. But, Rm. 5:8.
you can take that to the bank!!

I Said Yes to a Horrible Thing

My name is
and I am 39 years old. I have
been married for 17 years and
have 2 girls (ages 21 & 15 years)
old. I have been a happy and
content housewife & also a stay
at home mom for all of these
years. While in high school, I
occasionaly would drink a beer
or a joint every once in a
while but never liked it. At
age 35, my niece came up
to me and showed me a
drug. I had never really seen
drugs before and ofcourse I
was curious & very fascinated
by it as what I was told it
could do.

I didn't believe that
something could make you
so sexually fulfilled with
your partner & increase your
libido by 110 %. I tried
it - me & my husband, together.
I loved how it brought me &
my husband together sexually
& also just closer together as
a couple. I never knew
their was anything out there
that could make a person
feel that way. Began smoking

it and then IV use came into
play because I had watched
my niece + her husband do
it that way for one whole year.

The drug was Crystal Meth!
The day he stuck the needle
in my arm - was the worst
choice I could have made in
my life. - I just Never Knew -
- Curious - Curiosity got me.

Everything went downhill from
there. A life I never knew
existed - I was thrown into!
Once I started, I could not
stop until I just fell out.

I became a liar, a thief
and a felon within 4 years.
I never knew the power of
a drug. I had never done
anything but raise my 4 kids
+ love my husband. Why did
I say "yes!" to this horrible
thing. I just never knew!
I want my life Back now -
I'm ready - tried it on my own -
GOD is the only answer for me
to get the needle out of my
→

life. It is not who I am. This drug took all my morals & foundation away from me... I am here to reclaim what it took from me & my family?

Sincerel

This is the answer

I Said Yes To Everything

My name is Tom
and I'm currently Attending a Super Christian Rehab
center for Meth, Alcohol, marijuana pills. It is The Best
Thing I have done in my entire life. When I was Ten years
old my stepdad's brother molested me and my little sister
she was five years old. He would take me on Four wheeler
rides and would teach me. On Christmas That year my mom
asked me if he was doing anything to me he wasn't suppose
to. I was frightened and said no, on New years she asked
again. after a Couple of times of asking I finally told her The
Truth. she eventely brought me to The d.h.s office. After talking
to a representative They said They would Call us. After a Couple
of months They suppossably Called and my stepdad Answered
and didn't tell my mom.

About The Age of Thirteen I was in sixth grade
and I had a date to Homecoming dance, well before
That my sisters dad gave me two cigarettes and thats
when I started smoking. After Homecoming I smoked
went inside to give my Aunt A hug and kiss goodnight
she smelled The cigs on my breath I lied to her and
told her I didn't smoke but she knew I did. when my
grandma passed away I got mad at God and started
smoking pot I smoked pot a lot. when I turned 14
I cut loose and started drinking every weekend with
This guy who would buy all The beer and liquor you
wanted one Friday night about The time we were getting drunk
he said to me That he had A woman That came after
we go to sleep she comes and gives you oral sex, and
he asked me IF I wanted to partake me being naive
said yes.

A couple of years go by and I started To think (I've never seen This so called woman) I started thinking and it turned out to be him giving the oral sex But me Constantly wanting to party still kept going to drink I Just never stayed at This 37 year old man's house anymore. When I was 18 years old I started hanging out with an old school mate, one day he asked me if I wanted to go get Loratabs so I said yes and bought six of them, I kept eating pills until I didn't want to work at all. One night he asks me do you want to try some coke? I said yes and went to his Friends and bought an eight Ball We Continued to do this every weekend for six months. The night I quit I went to my moms I was drunk and had a long talk with her, my mother was more of a friend than a mom. Well I moved into A friend of a family's house We would drink and pop pills, smoke pot, my uncle one day came over and wanted to get crack. The friend Threw down some money and said you can go get it if you bring my friend back with you so I know you will Come back. We went and got it, They were Smoking when we got back, my uncle went to The bathroom and said, here, hit This, at that time was a bad time which led me spending 200$ A night on crack, I finally moved on from crack to meth. Meth is and was my weakness I was addicted to it for a year and a half I have teeth missing and two holes in my tongue and my family Thinks I was a drug dealer, They finally Convinced me to come to This rehab place. After I got busted, I said This is where my new born life started when I got There. I said I was mad at God but within A week God entered my life and changed The way I think, Talk, and act. I know God wants me to preach The gospel and he keeps reminding me, after all, I can do all Things Through Christ who strengthens me.

God has done so much for me it is Amazing I go to him before I do anything stupid like leaving. This is my testamony I hope you Enjoy it.

Sincerly
Tom
Age 20

I Screwed Up a Decent Life

Dear Hellfighters,

My name is ██████. I'm from ██████ (near ██████.) I have had a descent life by my family's standards. My mother was a single parent, but she worked hard to raise us. In school I was good at everything - sports, academics, arts, etc. My family always said I was smart and talented which, in their eyes, could only lead to success. During high school, I didn't do drugs, but I would drink a little. Alcohol was never a consistant problem, even as of late. High school flew by, and college was in my grasp. I moved to ██████, nine days after graduation to get a job and get familiar with the town. When school started, I was taking seventeen hours and working too much. I hadn't been home in almost three months, so I took a day off to go see my family and friends. When I returned, I was fired and couldn't get work, so I came home. Depression loomed, and my anti-drug attitude from before had diminished. One of my closest friends was developing a habit, and one day we decided to get some cocaine. From that day, I played with cocaine, crack, crystal, and weed. When I was nineteen, the work I was doing caused my back to give out. From then on, my main fix was pain-killers. Between coke and dilaudid, I was introduced to the needle. This was probably the worst thing that ever happenned to me. I continued to play with everything to take the edge off without physically having to do anything. My twenty-third birthday is near, and until about a year ago, I was on everything and nothing. My dad goes to a methadone clinic, and about this time last year, I began paying for his take-outs and getting part of them. About the same time, I realized that I could draw the liquid form of methadone and shoot it up. Since then my recreational drug use has depleted, but my habitual methadone use has been constant. I tried AA, about five months ago, but couldn't handle the detox, so I went back to the needle. It was about a month ago when my little sister showed up at my apartment saying that she talked to a friend ████████ whose family owns a treatment center ████████ and that I would get a scholarship if I went. I agreed to come without hesitation. God put this place in my path. I believe that if I go back to my old life, I will die. I'm in week one, and God has already worked miracles in my life. Thank you all for the work you do, and thank and praise God for many blessings.

Sincerely,

I Should Have Listened

To whom it may concern please understand please.

Dear Hellfighter,

My name is ██████ ██████. I would like to tell you a little story pertaining to two of your Hellfighters. I was ~~still~~ homeless about a year ago or a little more. I was going through some pretty rough times. Me and my family are not close at all and my girlfriend at the time was pregnant. I was very stressed out and wanted to escape so bad! I couldn't believe I was in a homeless shelter with nothing but a backpack full of stuff. I sat down to enjoy a free meal given to me by the grace of God, when I noticed two men sitting at the table. I said to them, I've never seen you two here before. They replyed well "We travel in our truck all around and spread the word of Jesus. Mind you at the time I've always believed in Jesus and God but I never was commited or wanted to be. So I said oh thats cool. They said to me that God wanted me to have this little booklet, ~~called~~ ~~its~~ with the Hellfighters crest on the cover. I took it and said thank you very much. They finished eating and left and I never saw them again. I cherished that little black book with the Hellfighter crest on it. I believe it had the new testament in it. Its been so long since I looked at it or had it in my possesion. Well any ways. to get back to the story ⟶

things got progresevly worse for me. Me
and my Girlfriend fought all the time.
The baby came and she wanted to give
him up for adoption. Her and her mother
fought against me about keeping him.
████ who was my Girlfriend said she
wasn't ready to be a mom and I had no-
one to stand by "ME" and help me keep
my son. Well I ██ ended up going along with
the adoption and afterwards I got addicted
to a substance along with my girlfriend.
Things got worse and we fought more and
I sanke deeper into depression and addiction.
I was put on probation for fighting with a
family member and violated 3 months later.
████ left me. My family has completly turned
their backs on me. I think about those two
men ██ who ██ are Hellfighters and I should
have listened. It was a message from God
himself. He was working through them. I am
now serving 9 months ██ in jail and I am
in the word of our lord now. God said. "If
you dont want to come to me on your own I
will bring you to me. Now I am in the word of
God reading the bible and ██ starting to
be the man of god I ██ have always been.
I would like to ask for another one of
those little black books with the Hellfighters
crest on it and anything else pertaining
to the Hellfighters. I would greatly appreciate any ██ info or books on the Hellfighters
because I would like to be one and do

consider myself one already. I hope my story hasn't offended you. I have asked Jesus to forgive me. I have read my salvation prayer. Jesus is in my life now. I have to keep him close to me. ~~Please~~ I am asking you please if there is any way I could get that little black book with the Hellfighters crest on it and any other ~~crest~~ Items pertaining to ~~the~~ the Hellfighters. I would like to also ask if there is any way you could send me a little bible. A small bible would be able to fit in my pocket and I could bring it were ever I go. Thank you so much Hellfighters. God bless you and I will pray for you. Please pray for me. If thier is anything I can do for you when I get out I will try my best. Here is my address and If it is possible I would ~~It~~ like to stay in touch with you seeming I do not recieve any mail or visits. except from Jesus. It would be nice to have someone to write to. THANK You

I am a Hellfighter!!!***

Sincerly

P.S. ~~███████~~
I would cherish any~~thing~~ pertaining to the Hellfighters. Keep up. I will keep bearing the standard for Jesus Christ our lord.

Dear

Sorry it's taken so long to write you. I am the only one answering the letters from all over the U.S. Don't get me wrong, I count it a Joy, honor & a privilege to do so. It's all for my LORD & SAVIOR JESUS anyway.

Hey, I've been in your shoes if you read my material I am sending you. Like me, you have to trust & wait on the Lord. HE will help you. I am a 51 year young minister for my Lord. YOU CAN BE ALSO. WAIT. Praise GOD for your salvation. (OVER)

152

ONE FREEDOM SQUARE   LAUREL, MS 39440-3367
PH. 601-649-1977   FAX 601-425-2411
email: hellfighters@headricks.com   www.hellfighters.com

Since you are a born

"ONLY THE BOLD WILL QUALIFY."

again Christian,
Just tell 1 person about
what Jesus has done for
you and guess what?
YOU are a HELLFIGHTER.
HALLELUJAH.

Write me
any time, my
Brother.   Phil. 4:8
We are
family. ☺
Love in Christ,   Robert A. Smith
                   Matt. 6:21
                   Ps. 147:3

HELLFIGHTERS
SEARCH & RESCUE

I Smelled the Stench of Hell

Hi! My Name is ███████ and I am writting you my testomoney of how I came ████ to Accept Jesus Christ As my Savior.

I was asleep in a jail and I haven't been in spirit with God for a very long time. I had had a dream that was so real a vision from God. I dreamed that I had died and when I stood in front of Jesus for my Judgement Jesus said to me go the other way for you have turned your Back on me Then I was falling in to a firey Pit my skin felt as if it was burnin I could smell flesh burning, hair burning. I could here people screaming Oh Lord forgive me. Then I woke up and realized I was still alive, I began to pray right there and the spirit of the lord fell over me. Now I have Jesus Back in my life and want people to hear my testomony. That it is so amazing of how Great our Lord

God really is. His never ending love
for us. I would like to become one
of his Hellfighters to wittness to
people for him. God Bless you.

I Sold My Soul to the Devil

My name is ███████ I was born &
raised in Jackson, ███. I am 3$
years old. I come from a church
going family but a very dysfuntional
family. My father was physically
abusive to me & my brother & my
mother was an adulterer.
My whole life changed at 7 years of
age. My mawmaw died and she was
my world. By age 11 I was drinking
& smoking cigarettes. My parents
divorced and the party was on.
I did very well in school and
continued to attend church. I
had a very rebellous spirit all
at the same time. I was pregnant
at 16 and gave birth to my daughter
at 17. I went on to attend
college with my daughter & her
father (my 1st husband) I thought
I was doing very well until
I started wanting to go out &
party, which led to my road
to full blown alchoholism
and becoming an adulter.
I graduated college and moved back to
MS. I divorced my husband & within

6 months I was engaged & married
again. the same destructive cycle
started. that marriage lasted 1 1/2
yr. Well going thru that divorce
I was introduced to crack cocaine
at the age of 23. ████████ I sold my
soul to the devil without even realizing
it. I went from having a beautiful
home, wonderful job, great mother, being a
to a hopeless drunk crack addict.
My mother court committed me
within 6 weeks. I was mad at the
whole world, I was in complete
denial. I was kicked out of rehab
the 22nd day and was high again
within 24 hrs. I moved to the Gulf
coast in ███, opened up my own
company, did very well for myself
relapsed in ███ again. Went to
the State Hospital for 45 days. During
all this time I was in & out of
jail constantly. I was so very
miserable. In ████ God blessed
me with a wonderful, healthy
baby boy. Only by the grace of God.
I was smoking crack when my
water broke, but he never tested

positive for cocaine. well after I
left the hospital with him life was
great. I was back in my church
& truly had a relationship with
God. Life was great. I was a leader
at Celebrate Recovery, was blessed
to attend the National CR convention
in ~~a~~ California. My little boy was
my best friend. well the economy
started going bad, MY company
was not doing good. I slowly
slipped back into the world. I knew
satan was grabbing at me ~~&~~ and
one day I finally gave in ~~████████~~
~~████████~~ My life immediately
~~was~~ went out of control.
My life was once A mess. then
one morning the police knocked on
my door just to ask me some
questions about a friend of mine
that was involved in a burglary.
well they knocked for 3 hours
with my little boy in the window
butt naked standing there with a
pizza cutter in his hand. I was
completely out of it coming
off of a crack binge. By the time

they kicked my door in DHS was there, my house was a wreck, they gave me a drug test of which I failed & the next thing I was putting the love of my life in his car seat in the social workers car and watching strangers drive off with my son. I thought I knew pain, but no I didn't even know the meaning of pain until I seen ████ Riding off & he had no idea that he would not see me. So then I tried to get it together & it was not happening I COULD NOT STAY CLEAN!
I knew that I was in the deepest Pits of my addiction. So on November 6 @ 11AM I came to the recovery center and I can truly say it was the best decision I have ever made in my life.

Thank You

I Took a Beating to Get to a Needle

Testimony or Story: I was 18 the first time I ever touched drugs and I was shot up with meth and cocaine by a sexual pretedor who was the director of the church camp I was attending for the past 5 years. During my last stay at the church camp, I felt God talking to me about reaching out to people I trusted and tell them I was batteling with Homosexuality. Well this camp director was in the group I di addressed and he told me he was a therapist and could help me with such feelings. The first time I went to his house we did therapy stuff but the 2nd time he got me drunk and shot me up with dope. I was instantly hooked and would do whatever for my fix. I would take daily beatings and sexual perveison just to get that needle in my arm. I did this for 2 years and God finally released me from that situation but by this time I was addicted. That was 12 years ago this Dec. I haven't shot up again until 4 weeks ago when I ended up in a coma! →

(use back of sheet if need

Mail to :   Hellfighter
One Freedom Square
Laurel MS 39440-3367

For the past 10 years I have been addicted to opiates and benzo's until 4 weeks ago when I met up with another guy. This guy was a lot younger than me, not like the other guy which was much much older, so I figured there wouldn't be any harm even though I knew he did drugs and was on the needle. Well one thing led to another and 8 days later without eating or drinking anything and not using the bathroom for the last 3 days, I was checked into the ER and my kidney's, liver, stomach and lungs stopped functioning. The ICU Doctor had to put me in a coma using profosol and ativan where I almost lost my life. They couldn't even do a brain scan to see if I was brain dead for 3 days because I still wouldn't stop moving. Well they finally did the scan and glory be to God there was no damage. A couple day's later I was fully recovered and completely healed, Thank you Jesus. Now I am at the Home of Grace getting help for my addiction and also what has happened to me. God is doing powerful things in my life and now I am a Son of God. I believe Jesus died on the cross for my sins just so that I can have eternal life if I believe only in Jesus christ. Thank you so much for letting me practice writting my testimony and being able to share it with you guys with all God's Love

I Tried To Kill Myself

Dear Brother/Sister

my name is ▓▓▓▓▓▓▓▓ a friend
of mine Here at the mission of hope
gave me a pamphlet of yours to read
and I found it very interesting. I would
like to share my testimony with you and
tell you how I ended up here and what
God has done for me. Since I have been here
I started drinking alcohol at a very early age
at first it was only on holidays that
my parents would let me and my 2 older
Brothers have a glass of wine. I liked the
way that it tasted and the way it made
me feel. By the time I was 12 years old
I was sneaking drinks all the time from
my parents liquor cabinet. at age 13
I tried pot for the first time and
enjoyed the way it made me feel also.
I always felt like I didn't fit in with
anyone at school so I drank more & more
at the age of 16 I dropped out of school
and went to work offshore with an
uncle. I made good money to much
for someone so young. Because with
money I discovered a lot more drugs
Cocaine Being one of these. I thought life
was one Big party. at the age of 19
I was married to a wonderful girl. she
didn't use drugs like I did but she
did drink every once in a while.
we were married for 5 years before she

Gave birth to our first Son.
2½ years later our 2nd Son was born
and in all this time I still continued
to drink alcohol and to use drugs
I didn't see it at the time but my
life was taking a downward
spiraling turn. I want go into any
war stories or drunk-a-logs but on
one of my many binges and many
Black out there was something that
took place in ~~my~~ lives that changed
me. I stopped drinking and using drugs
I did this for a period of 7 years
in that period our 3rd son was born.
I don't know exactly what happened
or why or when but I do remember that
all during that I felt like something
was missing. and I started drinking
again and it has only gotten worse.
I know that it had gotten worse
because on ▓▓▓▓▓▓▓▓▓ I tried to
choke the life out of my wife ▓▓▓▓▓
Because she told me she was leaving me
and taking our 10 year old Son with ~~her~~
her. I had up until that point never
laid a hand on her for ▓▓ years but in
a drunken rage I did this night and
ended up in jail. I called my boss
and he got me out. trying to kill the
woman that I love and going to jail

didn't slow my drinking down
at all. my wife and I separated
the same night I tried to kill her
this only added more fuel to a
hot, hot fire! Because you see
the more I drank the worse satan
got a hold on me. every day I
either planned ways to kill my wife
or thought of suicide. this continued
until may ▓▓▓▓ that was when I had
my last drink. for you see I had been
on a 10 day binge of alcohol and crack
cocaine use. When my boss who
is probably the best friend that I
have and my sister found me,
I didn't know it at the time but
they had been checking into rehab
centers to try and get me help.
when they called the mission of
hope they said I would need detoxing
before they could take me. I went through
that and the Dr's at U.S.A. Emergency
room told them if I hadn't came in
when I did I would not have lasted
another day. So God was looking out
for me even then. I finished the detox
program and came here on ▓▓▓▓▓▓▓▓
on the 25th of May I was saved. and
gave my life to Christ. since then
wonderful things have happened to me

164

I still have my job when I leave here. On Family Day I see my children when before they wouldn't have anything to do with me. My wife is even talking to me now although I don't know what the out come will be I can only leave it to Gods Will. Because my will & way didn't work Remember when I said something was missing in that 7 years I didn't drink or use drugs I figured it out since I've been here it was God that was missing all these years and I've finally found him and I'll never let go again.

Sincerely K

I Used to Drink A LOT

Dear Hellfighters,

My name is ████
From ████ Louisiana,
I am 47 yrs old and have been
struggling with sobriety for
many years — I am a chronic
alcoholic. Because of self destructive
living in my 20's (eating disorder)
and the onset of alcoholic
drinking around 35 yrs old
I developed a disease called
cerebellar ataxia — effecting all my
finer motor skills, walking,
speech and writing. With a few
weeks of sobriety I no longer
need my walker to walk and
I am able to write to you.

I have begun a long stay at
"████" in ████
~ a faith based rehab for
women. I have surrendered
to God — all my battles to fight
alcoholism have failed. I have
lost all — my health, most of my
family, my home. I pray to the
Lord my God to give me strength
→

MY LORD AND SAVIOR — AND to
OPEN MY HEART to HIS WORD.
I believe it WAS HIS WILL THAT
brought my to THE ████████ —
to STUDY HIS WORD, RECEIVE HIS
FORGIVENESS AND begin spiritual
HEALING.

To help with my studies could you
please send ME A Bible
IN LARGE PRINT

May the Lord bless you For All THAT you
give those seeking the LORD.

BLESSINGS

THOU GREAT THREE-ONE,
Author of all blessings I enjoy, of all I hope for,
Thou hast taught me
    that neither the experience of present evils,
    nor the remembrances of former sins,
    nor the remonstrances of friends,
    will or can affect a sinner's heart,
    except thou vouchsafe to reveal thy grace
    and quicken the dead in sin
    by the effectual working of thy Spirit's power.
Thou hast shown me
    that the sensible effusions of divine love in the soul
    are superior to and distinct from bodily health,
    and that oft-times spiritual comforts are at their highest
    when physical well-being is at its lowest.
Thou hast given me the ordinance of song as a means of grace;
Fit me to bear my part in that music ever new,
    which elect angels and saints made perfect
    now sing before thy throne and before the Lamb.
I bless thee for tempering every distress with joy;
    too much of the former might weigh me down,
    too much of the latter might puff me up;
Thou art wise to give me a taste of both.
I love thee
    for giving me clusters of grapes in the wilderness,
    and drops of heavenly wine
    that set me longing to have my fill.
Apart from thee I quickly die,
    bereft of thee I starve,
    far from thee I thirst and droop;
But thou art all I need.
    Let me continually grasp the promise,
    'I will never leave thee nor forsake thee.'

[159]

Dear

Been There, Done That! Man, I was 42 when I went thru the men's HOG in Aug. of '98. I had been for 10 years straight, drunk and stoned Every day. On one hand I can count the days I did not drink or drug. For 42 years I lived for satan, 25 of that in drugs & alcohol. When I came to the HOG in '98, they named me Shakey #2 cause there was already a guy there they called Shakey. My shakes were so bad I made a joke that you did not need a machine to mix your shake, just hand it to me, ha! Also, I could only put a little coffee in my cup or it would be on me instead of in me. On 4/20/99, this son of satan, ██████████, became a Child of the KING. I am now a 51 year young minister for my Lord. Give Him time to mold you into the beautiful new child that He wants you to be. Write me any time Robert A. Smith
Love In Christ, matt. 6:21 Ps 147:3

I Was On a 17 Year High

This is my Testamony.

I live in ████, Alabama on the ████ ████ Indian Reservation. I started out as a Child going to Church, with my Grandparent. As she got sicker I started not going like I should. Then I quit going all together. Started hanging out with the wrong Crowd. First came the drinking, when I got the hang of that. Then came the marajuanna I found out that you eat more, something I didn't want. I was already a big guy & didn't want to get bigger.

So I seen people doing Cocaine and I had to have some of that. Everybody said you don't eat on that. But as I learned over the years it was just a 15. minute high. Then came the Bomb I was introduced to Meth. It was a 17 year high for me. Started out just weekends, then over time. It grew to a 2 times a week & weekends. During that time I started losing weight. Then my wife started noticing the weight loss. Then, I wouldn't work like I was supposed to. Got behind on Bills, Got my first Felony. Ending up in Jail for 14 months. Got on Work release. But not like being with your Family Helping my wife with the children. And finally separting from my wife.

Going on now 3 years, From ████ to ████ I lost everything I had; Wife, House, Children & Vechicles. My Children will not even call me there Father. I lost all there respect. 2006 in Ended up back in Jail on a U. O. P.

I stayed 9 months & 9 days I asked my P.O.
about coming to this Rescue Center. He said IF
the Creek Indians said it was OK. He would not
go against them. Because I was already on Drug
Court with them. 2 years on a 1 year program.
So they agreed and here I am. By not completing
the 90 day Rehad, the Judge in my case would &
could give me a 10 to 20 year sentence. I wished
I could take it all back show my family really
what they meant to me. Only I can wait & see
what that will be.
    I know or I think I can right now only
God know's. Maybe my life can be restored my
Family will Forgive me and let's become one. In
the House of God I know now that's the only way.
I beleive in my heart I will make it here &
Become the man I was supposed to be For God
First then my Family. I Love my Family very
much. And I ▓▓▓▓▓ give my heart, Body & Soul to
Jesus. I know he will use me in a way that is
helpful to me, & my reward will be Eternal life
with him in Heaven.

    My Testemony.

170

THE WAY TO PERMANENT FAITH

"Indeed the hour is coming . . . that you will be scattered . . ." (John 16:32).

Jesus was not rebuking the disciples in this passage. Their faith was real, but it was disordered and unfocused, and was not at work in the important realities of life. The disciples were scattered to their own concerns and they had interests apart from Jesus Christ. After we have the perfect relationship with God, through the sanctifying work of the Holy Spirit, our faith must be exercised in the realities of everyday life. We will be scattered, not into service but into the emptiness of our lives where we will see ruin and barrenness, to know what internal death to God's blessings means. Are we prepared for this? It is certainly not of our own choosing, but God engineers our circumstances to take us there. Until we have been through that experience, our faith is sustained only by feelings and by blessings. But once we get there, no matter where God may place us or what inner emptiness we experience, we can praise God that all is well. That is what is meant by faith being exercised in the realities of life.

". . . you . . . will leave Me alone." Have we been scattered and have we left Jesus alone by not seeing His providential care for us? Do we not see God at work in our circumstances? Dark times are allowed and come to us through the sovereignty of God. Are we prepared to let God do what He wants with us? Are we prepared to be separated from the outward, evident blessings of God? Until Jesus Christ is truly our Lord, we each have goals of our own which we serve. Our faith is real, but it is not yet permanent. And God is never in a hurry. If we are willing to wait, we will see God pointing out that we have been interested only in His blessings, instead of in God Himself. The sense of God's blessings is fundamental.

". . . be of good cheer, I have overcome the world" (16:33). Unyielding spiritual fortitude is what we need.

APRIL 4

Write me anytime, my new
friend & Brother in Christ.
Love in Christ,
Robert A. Smith
Matt. 6:21
Ps. 147:3

Dear,

Man, I know you've 'lost' alot. But know this, my brother, "Behold, I AM the LORD, the GOD of all flesh: is there anything too hard for ME? Jer. 32:27. Also, Matt. 19:26, Mk. 9:23, Lk. 18:27. ~~~~~~ God can do anything, even restore guys like us. Also, He can restore families. I Jn. 5:14 "... if we ask anything according to HIS (will), HE heareth us." But, sometimes we have to go on to the next thing, sometimes, that door shuts, But GOD is the ONE who can Shut & OPEN! Trust Him, Pro. 3:5,6, Eph. 3:20, have faith, Heb. 11:1, Ex. 14:13, He will guide you, Ps. 16:11.

I Was On a Rampage

Dear Firefighters

My Name is ████████ Im 42years
of Age Im From Montgomery Alabama.
When I was 12 A Friend Invited Me
To smoke some Pot I Didnt Know much
About This but never the Less I started A
growing Addiction That changed My Life.
I smoked Pot on+off for 10years I hd Know
I deal my Life was going For The worsted.
At the Age of 22years old I entered a new
Addiction for crack cocaine my Life.
went to Levels I could never have Dreamed.
mixing All Addictions At once Pot Crack Pills
sex Alchole. I WAS in For The ride of my
Life. It wasnt Long. The ride Turned very
ugly And I was out of control scared Addict
Doing what Ever it took To Keep me At the
Level That my Life was At. I was on a rampage
$5000.00 - 2000.00 A day HABet This Took Me to
a new Level Know WhicH started Torches
Burning Every where. Famty - Love - Anger - Violent
Lycing - stealing - Jail - Committment - Mental Break
Marrige - Kids - I gAve It All up For The Drugs
At The Age oF 42year old Lost. with Blood
Dn my Lands on many diffrent times.
Broff knowing my Life From Min to Min
Deep in dedt to Drug Dealers scared Hidding
Pistol in my mouth crying so confussed
Hope was gone! But Once Again

Drug desler shows only to get my
Gun. for Drugs And To unArm me for
His Drug Dealing Friends I owe Thousands
of Dollars. There contract had Been
made. They were going to Take my Life.
I made my Last move. My Last week hidding
In A Hotel scared hungery and unArmed my no
gun. I had a pocket Knife and A ³⁴ Pipe 2 foot
Long. They Found me Last 2 Day They would
come 9-20 Times each day didnt anserew Door
Ever. 3.45 Am could not stand It no more
I could not Breath I pull All of The furitcher
Away From The Door And ~~coke~~ went out
I Looked All around Trying to get my
Breath weak From Hunger ~~scared~~ Lost.
All the suddon I heard 2 men Things
went very bad! very bad one man behind me
one man in Front my life came to This
I said god Help me. Now there going for Their
weapons. saying Again God I Dont want To Die.
I Knew if I Died That night I would go to Hell.
I'm ~~~~ Feghting for my Life. But I did not fill
alone. I AM now SAVED my Soul Belongs To god
And Ive Been Drug Free for Almost 1mo/wk
I never Looked Back to This city and never
Will. I will Live the rest of my Life
serving Jesus christ my savory. I was saved in
June   Praise god I never in the Last
20 years Felt The Peace or Love That Jesus

has Brout in To my Life Lord Thank you
for The Gift of Love.
HellFighters I never Knew how the Devil
or Evil spirets worked I Love Jesus.
And Living for my father King And Lord of
My Soul

I really Like what
HellFighter stands For

No Longer Lost

Found

174

A Prayer for a Clean Heart and Heavenly Wisdom

Strengthen me, O God, by the grace of the Holy Spirit. Make my inner self strong, and empty my heart of all useless anxiety and distress. May I not be drawn away by conflicting desires, be they worthless or prized, but may I consider them all as passing things and I too as passing with them. Nothing under the sun is lasting here where all is vanity and vexation of spirit. Oh, how wise is the person who thinks this way!

Give me, O Lord, heavenly wisdom that more than anything else I may learn to seek and to find you, to taste and to love you above all things, and to understand all other things as they are, as your wisdom has ordained them to be. Give me discretion to avoid those who puff me up with flattery and the patience to bear with those who work against me. It is great wisdom not to be tossed thither and yon by windy words nor to give ear to the falsely flattering serpent. May we each go confidently along the path he has started!

Write me anytime
Love in Christ
Robert C. Smith
Matt 6:21
Ps. 147:3

Dear ___,

Praise God that you lived long enough to make it to ▓▓▓▓▓▓▓▓▓▓ Man, the life of an addict or alcoholic is a tough life. Been There, Done That. I lived for satan for 42 years. I know. At 19, I assaulted police in Dallas. By the time I was 42, I was drinking every day, smoking pot every day, and doing as much 'nose candy' as I could get. Also, smoking 6 packs of cigarettes a day. I went to Home of Grace in Vancleave, Ms., a 13 week Christian rehab. I stayed 1 year. From 8/14/98, to 8/3/99. On 4/20/99, this son of satan became a child of the KING. I am now a 51 year young minister for my Lord. Wait for HIM to work in your life. HE WILL.

I Woke Up and She Was Dead

My name is ▓▓▓▓▓▓▓▓ and I'm at a Recovery Center for Men. I'm writing you to give you my personal Testimony. I grew up in ▓▓▓▓▓▓▓ parish Louisiana where I lived with my mother and uncle. The first Time I ever used drugs was when I was 13 years old. one evening a friend of mine came over and I snuck into my uncles closet and took a joint from his stach. We rode our bikes to The park and smoked The Joint. I remember I was so messed up I had to leave my Bike on The street corner because I couldn't ride it home. I ended up walking home That day. Thats all it took, I Loved weed and continued to smoke it for The next 5 years. At The age of 18 I started trying different types of Acid. This is when I met my First wife. I had shot up some Angel Dust and OD'd on it. She took me to The Hospital and took care of me during This time. I remember telling her "I'm going to marry you"! And I did. After This it was on. I started Deeling and using Coke, Weed, Quaaludes. I was still smoking weed everyday. I was also Drinking Heavy everyday. Many nights I would Blackout

and not remember anything That Happened. This
went on for years. I was still dealing +
using Coke, weed, pills and Drinking Heavily.
At The age of 35 I started using Heroin.
I divorced my first wife and married my
second wife on a bet. We were only married for
one year we were using Heroin together one Night
she went to sleep on The Couch and When I
woke up The next day she was dead she
had OD'd on The Heroin she had shot up.
After This I started sleeping around with a
lot of Different women. I was still Drinking
Heavy, still Having many nights Where I
Blacked out + passed out. Life was going
down hill fast. Everyday I was smoking
weed, taking Pills, shooting up heroin, snorting
+ shooting up Coke, Drinking Heavy. A lot
of This time was a blurr. I can
remember bits and pieces of days and
weeks. I was staying so messed up
all The time. At 38 years old I
went to make a deal to Buy some
Heroin, little did I Know That The
deal was being watched by The New
orleans police. I bought 17 bags
of Heroin. After I made The deal

and drove off. I noticed The police following
me so I stuffed all The bags of Heroin
in The AC vent. Well That didn't do
any good because They drove my car to
The police Department and put The Drug
dog in The car. They found The Heroin
and I went to Jail. I got off on
This Charge because They drove my car to
The police department My Lawer said They
planted it There. But This court Battle
cost me $18,000 dollars you would Think
I would have learned my lesson but I
didn't only Three months later I was
busted again With 7 bags of Heroin.
I went back to Jail again. While in
Jail I realized my life had gone
downhill and I needed some help.
When I went to court The Judge
reccomended a rehab. I found out about
This Recovery Center from a friend and
Now here I am. I've finally got some
Hope in my life Now, Through Gods
Grace I'm starting to feel better
about myself. I'm making a change
in my life for The good and I

feel like I'm going to have a good future
with God as my number one priorty in my
life. I'm finally feeling good for the
first time in years.   THANK GOD !

God Bless you
and please pray for me

I'm Glad I Didn't Jump

Testimony or Story: When I was 19 years old I was diagnosed with Crohns disease and was given Vicodin to ease the pain. I was addicted for many years until I met a woman who sold Cocaine and convinced me that it would numb my pain so I tried it and to my suprise it worked. I did that for 6 years until I was introduced to meth. I was addicted to meth for 10 years. About 5 years into my meth addiction I tried to commit suicide by taking over 200 pills. I was in a coma 4 over 8 hours and they did CPR on me four times. My Mom was one of the EMTs who took me took me to the hospital and performed CPR on me. They flew in both of my sisters from different states to say goodbye to me. You would think that would have made me stop but it didnt. I continued

its do imeth. And on May ████████ I was
up for 5 days and was tired of living my
my life the way I had and I found myself
on a Bridge in San Antonio Texas wanting
to end it and the cops stopped ██████ and
██████ Interstate and had a police helicopter
flying over. The last thing I remember
that stopped me from jumping was a
car had tried to help me before calling
911 and I was frantic and told them
to get away or I would jump. Before leaving
me I remember a woman yell at me
God Loves You! Not being a Christian I
didn't know how to take that. Two
police officers grabbed my arms just as
I was letting go of the railing. I was sent
to the State Hospital and begged my mom for help.
My sister found this wonderful place for me.
She lives in ████████ So here I am
by the Grace of God. Thank God for
his Grace. I now know that God is
the only Way!

I'm In Prison for Life

Dear Hellfighters

    I had the chaplin here at Pennington County Jail bring me a Hellfighters search and Rescue Handbook and this one is the property of PCJ and I would like To have one of my own and any information on your group. I would maybe have some help in prayer also even though I've been Blessed ~~████████~~ ~~████~~ haveing a life Sentance without Parole ~~████████████████████~~ ~~████████████████████~~ ~~████████████████████~~ ~~████████████████████~~ ~~████████████████████~~ ~~████████████████████~~

    I have had a Long road To where I am at this time of life, I am a Soldier for the Lord for many years I am 54 years "young" and Sometimes it shows. My road Has Had many trials and tribulations. there are times over these 54 years I've walked with christ and there are times I'Ue ~~o~~ walked alone and "Fell". This 10 years I've done in Prison has been the Hardest in life and no picnic. I before this always was a So called "Outlaw" Biker and I've ridden with friends in most Clubs all over (Germany, austrailia, and others). Here in States I've lived in Kansas, Texas, South Dakota (born), montana, and North Dakota. I've riden in or through all most all States and Hawi'l (Spelling wrong). The clubs I've been associated with in 70 SOS (Son of Silence) out of Denver Co. Banditoes Since 80's and Hells angeles in 90's and Banditoes, Outlaws

elfasaroes (Iowa), and many smaller groups.
I've never held a Club Patch To any club (gang)
and I've been ask by the best and the worst of
them. I have lived most of my life in   The West

I have had a hard life you could say. The
thing is though is that some one Has been takeing
care of my life and always come out after
a Down time. I lost my sight in my right eye in
1975 when I had a fight with a 16 penny nail and lost.
afte forcably removing nail I was Totally blind
                and still am in Right eye. I still
Have the eye even though I Pulled nail out myself
with others on the Job holding Head still which
Saved the eye eve tho the many stitches and 2 different
sergery's on left eye I have been Blessed with
my sight for all these years.
   I've Had 6 different Bike accidents and
always walked away after except 1 Where
Right leg was pinned between Bike, and car
and still pins, nuts Bolts, and faith along with
8 months of recovery (1   ) I don't even have
a limp Plus 3 seperate Breaks and Some how healed
up well. There are many incidents in my life
That I should of died but I didn't except
at 9 years old was totally Flatlined for
1/2 hour but Father, old army WWII vet wouldn't
allow his Birthday Present   (me) to stay
dead and there have been many things in life
I wondered about, but there are somethings
That Pops say's is a gift from God.
   Well enough of that and there is alot more
To that story and my life that have to do with

wondering spirits as my 57 year old sister
Tells me (Babtist). I came from a line of
Christian people and all my sisters
all are devoted ~~Baptists~~. Baprist ▓▓▓▓
we were Brought up Lurthern.

I know I went off on some of my early life
and stuff. I have had as sister says wondering
spirits and as I got older and I never Drank
But had a constant smoking habit that seemed
To mellow the things I've seen and felt. I
over the years allways Been a bike mechanic
and have had major People I've associated
with and mechanised on their Bikes from 1980's
to now I've always had The name (wrench)
Tacked to me and was given this name at Sturgis
Drag Strip By a Pres. of one of the biggest Clubs
in the world. ~~Ihave~~

I've had prison Time starting
SD, Then recharged ~~i4~~ Federal charge,
and while Still in custody Rechared wit
RICO and Threatening, Federal, witness, illegal
use of (Jail) phone and conspiracy. I never
had anything on record Till 1989 and 3
Felonys later!... I was released from Federal
Prison Camp, and Clean with faith, and said
That after opening Bike Shop that I would
never go to prison again, and believed
my self.

My establishment was Called ▓▓▓▓ Repair and
it got so big in 2 years that I Bought a huge
Building and offered others partnership
if they worked Shop and well ended up
with 2,600 floor shop space and 900 showroom ⟶

and no one to assist and I just worked in the
Bike, machine, (cnc) shop, and Paint shop. With
1 Painter and Partime help mechanics and Bookeepers.
The thing in shop was I catered To The
Broke those who really couldn't afford much
and had one bay where anyone to save
money could work on their own bike I as
The machinest and overseer. Had room in Back
I also stayed in.

any way as things went became way to
big for one owner.

In July in Jail and Prison for life
without parole. Then The shop was produceing
The fat tire cycles before there were any Jesse James,
OCC choppers and Billy lane.

now in prison again for life I was able To
see all my old friends   they
where Just older and as my old fall partner
in prison one the orientation video was
a ex Hells angel called "Dirty al" who I was
charged with in   for drugs. The guy
was the guy in orientation video telling
The new inmates about the "Hill" Granite
city and if one needs to do their own
Time and To not take, Borrow, or accept things
from inmates because one could have
other intensions and best be left to do ones
own time.

now there is nasty al from L.A. telling
everyone about How it is and a old friend
That now had white goatee and earing in
Left ear of a cross and Pierced hole in
middle bottom lip. I then Knew That

Life couldn't be that bad doing life
in prison it was just that my latest
son was only 1 year old, and 2 other Boys
and 1 girl that was hard to live with
as who I am, The one taking care of my own.

I go to first church service in orientation
on thursday night and I get to see my old
friend AL (Dirty AL) in Boots 1 spur (which he always
wore) vest earing, and I give the hug
of friendship we have, and sit and
wait for service to start. The guy at the
pulpit is talking about how he is glad everyone
was there, and we do song and after this
inmate participation "I Love Jesus I really
do, I Love Jesus How Bout you" and about
only half of the congergation Responds
with the same until it's a yelling match
for Both sides, and gets everyone to
participate.

Now after more song and prayer
the guy at the pulpit comes accross
with how he lived life, and how he knows
people in the audience that he hasn't seen
for awhile plus about life, and his
life of being saved, and I get
drawn into all this by the guy at the
pulpit who at the time was a CMA
(christian motorcycle Associate). This guy
keeps bring up his past, and How it was
and how it is now. I am truely believing
in this guy the chaplin at the
pulpit, and I know that I believe I Just
need more faith, and belief

in Jesus christ and Holy spirit, even though
I'm in prison for life, and I know I didnt
deserve what happened to me. The chaplin
ends the service with song, and prayer then
call to alter for believers which I've always
if I can go for prayer, and I aproach
The chaplin (pastor AL   (Dirty AL) who
we pray together.

  Now AL is over the years now a Pastor
of his own church and has been in penticostal
and other religious magazines for his ministry
call now, "Set Free ministrys" in Sioux Falls
S.D.

  This was 10 years ago and my prayer and faith at times
had been none existant in prison be cause Ied watch guys
 stealing, assault guys, and do many things and
then go to service and act like they were Holyer
Than anyone. this made me become a "Cell" christian
and on weekend fellowship 2 days 3 times a year
I attend with CMA and set free ministry s praise
and worship (pastor AL) and I out 4 sundays I would
attend when it was AL's week for sunday service
and after years of AL saying that "Wrench you need
To keep the faith and so you will get out again so
you can join our praise and worship group." Well
          my coviction was vacated and I
know it was devine intervention that has
gotten me this far and I ask who reads
This to keep my Situation in prayer
so I may be free at last. Well I could be
free and working if I had 1 mill in rediculous
Bond set. yes I have been Bonded on 50 thousand
cash and then recieved a misdameaner

and recieved more press as att. Says
more than the Govenor and President
put together. He also at Bond hearing
for misdameaner 1 mill bond. Wrench Lets
Just get pur pocket change out you should
have a mill, maybe I do he says and
I say Judge for real, she says 1 mill next
case. So I was out 18 days in 10
years on 50 thousand and women Judge
gave 1 mill bond on top. Ross has a Bike
Shop he opened with my old parts and stuff
from old shop I gave him power of att To
get and start shop in ████████ with parts
and all. Not worth 1 mill yet about ½
and we also do salvage Bike and crushing
car Bussiness, and trucking but trucks used
To haul crushed cars only now. Well I made
a long short letter and excuse the mispelling, long
sentances, and sloppyness. Bye for now.

Friends To The End
God Bless

I'm Struggling

HELLFIGHTERS,

My name is ████████ and I recently had a chance to check out the Bible "Hellfighters" in a Bible study I joined in "Washington, County, Arkansas" in a "Adult detention center" (Jail). I was amazed at the personal stories that I read inside!

Wow! It made me realize that there is hope for me after all! Never, have I felt so understood ... not alone. I am but a baby in Christ and have just recently turned my life over to God. I am going back to prison for the 8th time in the last 15 or 16 years.

I'm an addict ... have been for most of my life now. I am a junkie of methamphetimine. I have lied, robbed, cheated, stole and disobeyed God and went against his word over and over again. I am finally tired of my life and want change more then ever!

I want a Christian life ... a life ... to be a man ... a God fearing man! Not only for myself but for my fiancee and altogether 8 children. I pray constantly for help...for his will to be done! To be the man he wants me to be for once.

But I can't do it alone and I know this. I need all the help I can get. Prayers ... prayers ... prayers! Part of the reason I am writing this is to ask for a Bible, please? And pamplets you may have on prayer and becoming a Christian ...

Any literature really and Bible studies as well. Please, help a struggeling man in any way you can, please? And to thank you for the encouragement your stories and your Bible gave me! Please, pray for me and my family and keep doing what you are doing! Amen...

If your able to help me with literature ... and or a Bible and or Bible studies then please wait a few weeks from this date ████ 10 and mail anything that you have to :

As I am waiting extradition to yet another jail. I want to thank you for your time and understanding and I'll keep you in my prayers..

Struggeling

God Bless You!!

I've Been Addicted All My Life

My name is ███████
and I'm currently at a Christian
Recovery Center for Women.
Thank God I made it here!
You see, I grew up really
fast and with a very crazy
home life.
My mom & dad divorced when
I was seven. Mom's an
alcoholic & was very, very,
physically abusive.
I quit school at 15 yrs old,
was a mom by 16. I had
a horrible fear that I would
abuse my kid too, so when
he was █ months I sent him
to a relative to be raised in
a better atmosphere.
After that I was full of
anger and pain and didn't
know how to stop it, so a
couple months before I
turned 17 I tried heroin;
I'm 36 years old now and
have been an addict all

my life. I never thought
I'd quit (never wanted to)
until resently.
In April my brother was
killed and every thing since
then has led me, a step at
a time, to this place where
I can finely start over,
with God in my life instead
of pain, anger or drugs.

God saved me for something
and I'm very excited to
find out what that is.
I've been clean since
July 9th of this year for
the first time ever and
I pray several times a day
for God to show me, teach me,
and fix me a little more.

Sincerely

It Blowed Me Up

Hello People

My Name is Keith ▆▆▆▆ I was Born in ▆▆▆▆▆ My parents were good to me, when i was 6 we moved to ▆▆▆▆▆. I went to 11th Grade, I smoked my first Joint when I was 13. When i was 14 I was Drinking smoking Pot. Hanging around the neiba Hood, out lauz. When i was 16 I was saleing Pot at school. most of my friends alluayz came By on Weekends Buy pot. A LB of pot Back then was $120.⁰⁰ $15.⁰⁰ a Bag. I quit school and started shrimping on Big Boats in the Gulf. I then met some peoples from Key West fla. I would Haul poundn' of Pot from Key West to Mobile on shrimp Boats. so when i was 22 yrs old I would ride from Key West to panama canal and get tons of pot 100 LB Bale. 13 of us got Busted in panama with 20 ton, Aboard ▆▆▆▆▆. the federal government served 3 indictments on me aiding a abetting, Rackateering, Conspracy to import maryjaw into the united states. I took a plea Bargain and was sentenced 5 yrs in federal prison, 19▆▆ I was sent to tallahasee FCI. 1989, I met Rev Jim ▆▆▆ I was shipped to lexington Ky, and then shipped to ▆▆▆ texas. I never testafied against anylady. I got out in ▆▆▆ got a job 2 yrs after my release I was Back to selling pot lortalz valijm what ever i could sale to make a dollar. 10 yrs ago I was introduced to crystal meth. and yes my know it all me learnt how to cook meeh. I got up with some people that

Had the recipe Hitler used. It sold forth
about a month ago my nephew and 2 of his
friends tryed to cook and got Blowed up
a week later my nephew ████ ████ Died
at USA Burn unit in Mobile ala. the other 2
are still in Burn unit, I feel so Bad, I Wish
now I would have led them to church.
now I am strictly against it, I found Jesus
here at the Recue Mission, God has Kept
me alive all these yrs. for some reason.
I pray law enforcement Will crack down
& stricter prison terms, I do Believe the
government Has a ████ ████ ████
to detect meth labs. I really think the
government are doing their Best to stop
this serious Problem. I Will Do all my Best
to help them track Down these EXACutioners
and out to Destroy peoples lives, I was lucky
16 yrs. and I feel God Would Bless me for
looking out for his children, I hear a lot
about you people God Bless you people
I love you.

         God Bless

It Started Out Soooo Slow

My name is : ▓▓▓▓▓▓▓▓ I'm 31
yr's old. My parent raised me in
a Christian home. I've always had a pretty
easy life. Played sports + always used the
Charm + innocents that God gave me to
fool the world. It started out in High
School when I was winning all the girl's
hearts, because I was the pitcher of the
High School baseball team. Also one of
the better wrestler's in High School. One
of the better Widereceiver's there. I
loved to dance and was good at it to.
God gave me all these talents +
I used them for the wrong reasons. I thought
my life at the time was going excellent,
but what I didn't know is it was going
straight to Satan. It all started out so slow.
By just going drinking one time, having premarital
sex, smoking one joint, watching t.v. shows that have
wrong doings in them, M.t.V., music, andso on.
There's soo many things I didn't know lead to
sin that I didn't knew about. But young
me thought I knew everything.
I joined the Army to try + get away from
it all + start over. But that didn't work
because I was not ready to change yet.
So I kept going down the same road of insanity.
Ended up spending 5 yr's in the Army and got kicked
out for drinking. Then when I got out of the
Army I met a wonderful women, and I thought
that would change my life. But it didn't
It seemed like I was looking to fill my heart
but I kept trying the wrong things to fill it.
So I thought maybe a kid would change
it.

So me and this woman had a daughter.
It was excellent. But then of course
the round Robin that I was in kept
on having to complete it's circle. This did
not work either. So I moved on but
kept in touch with my daughter. But was
not a good father to her. I wish I
could do alot of things over I missed
the first part of her wonderful life.
The only time I would get with that
part of her time. Then I met another
woman so I got married to her
she was beautiful, I thought I had
the catch of a lifetime. She was perfect
in all way's she had a daughter too. So
we spent our time with our kids. When
we weren't with them we were drinking
+ partying together we like the same
music. We had the same plan's for life
also wanted the same things out of life.
We both wanted a son ▬▬▬▬▬▬▬
▬▬▬▬▬ I thought this would be
it. Then I would straighten out and live
for God. So for the first 2 yrs. I did
we had a beautiful son. I toll God +
made alot of promises that I would
quite drinking also alot of other things.
I would do it for a little while until
My body or my personnel will could not
do it any longer. Then not wife started
drinking together heavily + stopped going
for our goals. Then I cheated on my wife
because I thought she was cheating on
me. My whole life was turning upside down

again. Then I started getting into trouble with the law all the time. In ~~the~~ the yr. of 2, ▮▮ before I met my wife. I got lured into a room by a woman when I was drunk. ▮▮▮ When I got into the room I got beat & hit by a crobar & duck-tape from head to toe. From then on every time I would get really drunk I would Black-out. If someone pushed me around or got me in a corner when I got drunk It's like I would go into a defense mode. Very scary situation. But anyways as my story goes on. I ended up in jail was doing ▮▮▮▮▮▮ 7 mnths well I did that little bit of time. Ended up talking to the Lord why I was in there promised him a bunch more things while I was in there. How I would not do drugs & drink anymore. I was going to straighten out as soon as I got out. Well I found out God does not like to be used. So I got out for 21 days ended up catching some pretty heavy charges. this time. ▮▮ They where going to give me 6 yrs. In the state pen. I prayed & begged God to forgive me & Thank ▮▮ God ▮▮▮ He does have Mercy, and he does forgive. I ended up doing 9 mnths in jail. The Judge goes to ▮▮▮▮ with my parents. So I ended up getting 6 mnths in a Cool Recovery Facility But while I was in jail. I was mad at the whole world so I ended up fighting alot. Ended up in Maximum security. A 6 x8 cell with only me in it. Also a Bible, and a t.v. That had ABC CBS, NBC, Day Star, Christian Channel.

I've never been locked up all alone.
At first it was the most terrible thing In
the world I'd ever been, also very lonely.
But eventually It was the best thing that
ever happen to me. I started reading the
Bible and praying alot. At first I seen
no change then after about a month or so
in there by ~~myself~~ myself and getting a
~~pattern down~~. Also starting really pray with
alot of conviction on my heart everything
around me ~~started~~ to change. People in the
jail that I didn't like I ~~started praying~~
for them instead of getting mad at ~~them~~.
They all started being nice to me ~~and~~ instead
of arguing & ~~fighting~~. It was getting easier
& easier to just be nice to ~~people~~. Then
I accepted the Lord. God gave me a
taste of what It could be like to be a
Christian. It was all starting to make
sense. Also I started having that inner
piece. I finally ~~a~~ filled ~~my~~ empty
Heart And all I needed was the Lord.
Thank God for Trials that he puts
me through. He finally brought me to
the Light. Now I got so much work to
do I have a short time on earth. I
have my whole family & alot of friends
to bring back to the Lord.

Love

It's Not Easy To Run and Hide

Hello   DEC, 11th

FIRST OFF God bless you All!

IM ███████████ .. I was

WRITTING The RING man...

Im Not sure if you remember

me. I was WRITTING you from

A PRISON IN ██████ , CA.

FOR A WHILE. Well Now im

IN ████ , CA.. ON A violation

For Abscounding. I Ran From

Parole ... I Ran From California

TO Arizona where my mom is!!

The Reason that I Ran is; me

And ████████ GOT INTO A big

ARGUMENT over dRugs...

I Guess while I was iN Prison

Some dude was GIVING her

dRugs, And She was STRUNG

OUT ON meth when I GOT home!

I KNOW IT takes Two BUT **He**

Should have KNOWN The Consiquences.

Well ANY ways I wANTed her To

Tell me where he was So I could

Get AT him iN The Alley FOR

A second TO EXPlain why you

dont mess with A MANS LAdy!

Well MY TEMPER FLEW!! She

didn't give him up because
she didn't want problems..
I did NOT hit her RINO !!
I grabed her by her arm
though when she turned her
back on me !! And shook her
like a rag doll... I realized
I was making a mistake,
And appologized then took
her to her moms house....
After that I went to my friends
for the night.. I wanted to
see her so I went to her
friends house ████████ that night !
I have no problem with ████
I never have... But its her
brother that gives ████
the drugs his name is
█████ - well RINO I went
to ████████ house, And the
lights were on so I knocked,
And No one answered so
I jumped the fence And
tapped the window.. The
lights went out so I
jumped the fence, And

WENT TO THE FRONT door AGAiN,
Deb ANSWERED ANd I
ASKed FOR ████████ ... She
said That "I WARNed YOU
That I was CALLiNG The COPS"
I RepLied "What? NO YOU did
NOT, Why ARe YOU doiNG That !!
WheReS MY WiFE"!! She was
ON A cell Phone SAYiNG "Some-
ONeS BReakiNG iNTO MY house
ANd he has A WeaPON !!" So
I WALKed back TO MY CAR,
ANd LeFT back TO MY FRiENdS.
The NeXT MORNiNG I WeNT
TO MY house TO GeT MY
CLOTheS TO GO TO MY MOMS
iN ARiZONA. TheN TWO COP
CARS CAMe AROUNd The
CORNeR. I WAS OUT FRONT
bY MY CAR. TheRe WeRe TWO
COPS. I WALKed UP TO The
FiRST ONe ANd iT WAS A
FeMALe. She said Who ARe
YOU So I said MY NAMe,
TheN She said "Oh We've beeN
LOOKiNG FOR YOU MR.

Put your hands behind your
back!!" So I did!! Rino!
I don't know what I was thinking
but As soon As she Grabbed my
wrist I twisted Around. And
yanked my Arm from her
Grasp, And took of running!!
I escaped And eluded Them
And Hid-out untill dusk! ~They Impounded my car.
Then I went to the Grey hound
Bus station, And took the
First one Smoking to Arizona..
I talked to ████ And She
was Sorry that It All happened
And came to Arizona The next
week to see me. We made up
but I knew I was in trouble!!
I Thought the worst!! Bra
I was scared!! She said
████ called And Reported
And the cops Questioned
her!! She said I didn't (Told the cops)
hit her but I Grabbed her
wrist. They took pictures
of The mark.. So I Got
even more scared!! but

No WARRENTS FOR MY ARREST
come up though!! ONLY
The P.A.L. WARRANT "(ParoLee
At LARGE)" SO I was Like
whats UP. Then I GOT PULLed
over IN ████████████.(About
████ Min. From LAUGHLIN
Nevada). STILL NO other
WARRENTS Though RINO..
That was November 8th
They EXTRIDITE me back
to CALIFORNIA. RINO This
whole time IM PRAYING
BRO!! PROMISSING The WORLD
you know The same old STOREY!
But FOR some RESON RINO MY
heart MENT IT! I didN'T
INTEND FOR IT TO Go down
Like IT did! I was ON The
Run
I WANTED TO TURN MY SELF
iN Every day! I was So
Ashamed That I blew IT!
I. Hurt My WIFE So bad
And OUR baby evenMORE!!
I PRAYED FOR ANSWERS (I

Trulley had Faith That If
I Put it into Gods hands I
would be ok!! That's when I
Got busted!! I Sat in Chino
For A Couple of weeks And
kept my Faith And Prayed
Im STill Praying! I Talked
To Loren
And She Told me That There
were New warrants out!!
3. of Them! I wasn't Shocked
I knew it was Comming!!!
She didn't understand The
Charges in detail but She
Said "Something with A cop,
And what I did To her And
Deb "!! So I asked her
To Print it out Please, And
To Give me your Address
So you can help me out Spiritually
Because I Still have my
Hellfighters Bible AT home!!
Well Today I Got A Letter
with your Address And
The Charges!! Im Not Shure
If Their Felenes or Mistimener

204

If you have time can you
please look them up in the
California penal code book?
→ count (1) PCM 273.5 CA)
→ count (2) PCM 148 CA) (1)
→ count (3) PCM 664/602.5 CA)
  I have put it in Gods hands
already... R'no what I did was
wrong I broke the law! Mans law
is Gods law!! I was and am wrong!!
R'no I have aske for forgivness!!
I deserve to be punished! but
Bro I want to be with my family
so bad... I'm ready to do my time
though... right now I habe to
do my prison violation for
absconding then go to county
for court... I was told that
my charges are misimener!
If thats true my prayers are
answered God willing!! but
like I said R'no I've put it
into Gods hands. And I do feel
blessed!! If you can please
pray for me and my wife. And
baby! Lorava got laid of last
month... can you please send
me another Hell fighters bible
I love it and miss it! ld!!
I feel terrible about reitting
to you this way but I dont

KNOW WHERE TO TURN AND
your the GODlyest MAN I
KNOW RIGHT NOW!! you helped
MY MIND REST BEFORE YOU
TRULLEY are A blessing
TO me AND YOUR MINISTREY !!
Any help that you Can offer me
will TRULLEY be A blessing!!
Thank you bro!!
I TRUST YOUR ADVICE!!

GOD BLESS
YOU ALL!!

I TRUST AND believe IN The Lord!! I have
FAith it will be All Good!! I'm IN GODS hands Now!!

Jesus and Home of Grace
Will Change Your Life

My name is ████████, I am
fifty years old. I am from ████████.
I have three sons and a daughter, three
grandsons and a step grandson.

I have been here at, The Home of Grace
since Nov.██

I have been struggling with alcoholism
all my adult life, Well if you call eighteen
an adult. I had turned my life over sto the Lord at
one point of my life. During the time I
was pregnant and my children were young.
Then I back slid, my marrage ended.
Thats when I started drinking again.

Its the same story as any other ~~alcolic~~
alcoholic. The use of Alcohol destroyed my
marriages (that I had attemped, for the wrong
reasons.) It destroyed relationships with
family and friends and worst of all, it stole
so much away from my childrens childhood,
Something, I can never make up to them.
Through it all, we were always close.
There were times that they would get angry
or hurt with me ~~sometimes~~, but they
always let me know that they loved me.

After they were all grown, my two
younger boys got addicted to pain pills.
So ofcourse, I blamed myself, so I had
to drink alittle more to drown →

out the guilt I was feeling.
(my sons) I checked into some rehabs for
them and found out about thier missions
I was also thinking about it for myself, but
they didn't know it.
Thank God, they were both ready to get
help at the same time. We brought
them the same day and they were
together through the whole program.
They both had alot of support from the
family. On the last visitation, before
their graduation, one of my sons pulled
me to the side and said, mama, you
need to go to this Recovery Center
It will change your life, I promise.
They both said other things about how
it helped them. They didn't have to say
anything, I saw what it did for them.
I had all my paperwork already done,
but still wasn't sure if I wanted to
go for that long. Until my one son
said what he did about it changing my
life. God did something to me right then
when I heard those words. And I knew
I wasn't going for them, I was going
for that changed life, they were talking
about. ⇒
    They graduated Oct 30 (Fri), I came
here Tues. Nov 13th. Today makes 30 days
Sober for me. Thank you Jesus.
God is just been working miracles
Miracles in my family's life.

I have been getting cards and letters from other family and friends, who I haven't talked to for quiet awhile. They are all being supportive and encourging. They are even telling me what a testimony I am to them.

By the way, my boys are both doing great. They were both able to go right back to work. All of my children have grown of closer ~~together~~ and they're all making sure mama has everything she needs. We are all looking forward for my graduation so we can spend time together sober, like a real family and try to catch up on so much ~~we have~~ missed out on.

I know this was only suppose to be a short ~~testimony~~, but I get so excited about what God has done and is still doing in my life I just want to go on and on.

On the following page is what I wrote one of my sons today.

Today

I am not the same person I was before
I came here.
I feel so good, happy, and blessed
I can walk with my head lifted
high and not be ashamed.
I don't have to wake up in the morning
with a hang-over, not wanting to get
out of bed, because I had no reason too.
I don't have to beat myself up all the
time, with the guilt of what a mess
I made of my life and my childrens.
I don't have to get drunk anymore
to ease the pain I was feeling inside.
I don't have to feel like a nobody
anymore, because I am somebody.
I am a child of God and He loves me.
He will never leave me or forsake me.
"I am nothing without God!"

I almost forgot what I was writing this
for. I would so much appreciate one of
your bibles and a tee shirt, size Small.

Thank you and God Bless
Sincerely,

Dear Hellizgn,

I am currently an inmate at ▮▮▮ Warriors Correctional Center in ▮▮▮ Oklahoma. This is my third year of a ten year sentence. I am in prison because of Meth. I am 49 years old with two grown children. I have been happily divorced for 12 years. Which is about when I started using Meth. At first I just used Meth to have a little buzz. Then, I used Meth to get me through the lonely days. Then I used Meth to get me through the pain of the lonely days. Then I used Meth to just get me through the days. Soon, I allowed other people to cook Meth in my garage. Then one day a "friend" showed me how to cook Meth. I never cooked a lot of Meth, only about an ounce or so at a time. Next thing I knew I had no job, Meth was my job. It gave me the lifestyle I thought I wanted. I could do as I pleased, whenever I wanted. After 17 years of marriage this was very liberating. (I thought) After a couple years of Meth supporting me, the police finally came knocking on my door. By this time I had pushed everyone in my family away from me except my youngest son. I left him all my responsibilities. At 18 I thought he could handle it. Bottom line was he couldn't. I had embarrassed him. He came to see me in jail once, I had to tell him his mother was going to prison for 10 years. That was the last time I had contact with him or any of my family for over a year. After a year my dad and I started talking and him and my step-mother have been very supportive. Last December I saw my only sister for the first time in 7 years. Last April of ▮▮▮ while I was in lock I had a lot of time on my hands and the only book around was the Bible. I read it cover to cover. There while I was in lock I asked the Lord for forgiveness and to be my savior. At that moment I became a different person. A better person. Jesus leads my life and I have never felt so free. People that I knew before I was saved tell me that I act and look different. What a compliment to God.!! He has made me whole!! It is still difficult at times being in prison, but I have JESUS to help me through. My youngest son finally wrote me last September. He said he loves me and he had joined the Army. We wrote a few times and then my letters were returned as unknown. I guess he shipped out. I worry like crazy, but God told me he would take care of him. I took your METH addiction class last November here in ███. It was one of the best and most informative classes I have taken. Keep it up! Another inmate who also took the class told me that you sent her this small Bible and also a T-shirt to her house. I would like to request a Bible

Thank You,

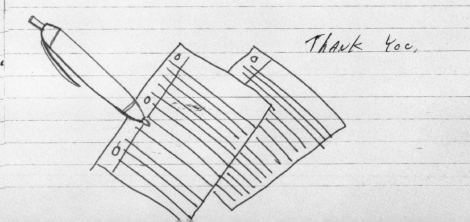

Love Makes You Do Things

Name: _____
PLEASE PRINT: (first)   (last)

Graduation Date: ████████████████   ████████████
The Lord works in mysterious ways, but GOD is good! =)

Testimony or Story: My whole life I have struggled with serving the Lord. When I was 8 years old I remember being slapped in the face for saying I do not believe in GOD, and it shook me to the point of rejecting him and all of Christianity for many years. At 15 I started drinking by consuming Vodka and I took to alcohol immedietly. I started smoking cigarettes at 16 and by 18 was smoking Marijuana which became my DOC* for many years after that. I struggled with Alcoholism and addiction in general my first semester in college at Southern Mississippi (USM) and was in Bradford rehab before my second semester. Got out 28 days later. Stayed clean for awhile, but was turned back onto Marijuana and my addiction got worse. I wound up back in Bradford for about 14 days and when I got out I spent over a year doing nothing. I chose to go to ████████ University's ██████ program after awhile. My first day in ████████████ FL I was arrested for possession of Marijuana and drug paraphenalia. Bailed myself out, got a lawyer and it seemed to take care of itself over time. Before probation (3 months) was over I started back on marijuana and used it all through my

(use back of sheet if needed)

Mail to :   Hellfighter
One Freedom Square
Laurel MS 39440-3367

*Drug of Choice

education. When I went back home I was depressed all the time. I drank and smoked like it was going out of style; until I was arrested again. This time it was paraphenalia, possession of Marijuana and a DUI. After 2 weeks in jail, mostly spent in Suicide Watch, I got out and did 9 months of probation. I got involved with a girl I liked from the first time I met her. I grew to love her but she hurt me so often my drug use once again increased, heavily. I couldn't deal with having my heart crushed over & over again and just when I thought things were going to turn around after they were at their worst she told me she was leaving; moving to Las Vegas. The week before I had put my arm through a window causing a large crippling injury which left a nasty permanent scar which she was apart of; though it was noones fault. I was told I would get closure which I was denied, but I wished her off well, with love, immedietly falling to pieces when she pulled out. I thought I could drink away that pain. Upon (quickly) realizing this wouldn't happen, about a week, I decided a vacation in California might cheer me up. I left with a friends wife, got abandoned, and just wandered on my own a few days. I was offered a trip to Vegas to party, got hustled, wound up alone. Decided to go anyway and visit my ex. Wound up housing her for weeks with me in a hotel, kicked her out for running off on me. She crawled back, promising me we would try to better our relationship and our lives. I wound up getting us an apartment and quickly found myself addicted to SPILE and bath salts. I couldn't seem to maintain her affections or attention. She would dissappear on me all the time, which threw me into a spiral of anger and ever increasing drug use. I wound up being arrested twice for Domestic Violence, both times only receiving disturbing the peace. By then I was using 5-10g of SPILE a day on top of 1-2g of bath salts through inhalation, a day. I one day called my Dad to say goodbye; I committed to suicide. Was picked up by an ambulance and placed in a Psych ward. My dad flew to Vegas and offered to bring home to get help, so I left a place & a woman I loved, promising to return. When I realized it would take a long time, I tried to get her back home as well because she had fallen prey to Crystal Meth. When it got bad enough, she agreed and her parents brought her back. We committed to better our relationship. Eventually I felt I was the only one working at it and got back on SPILE while supporting her drinking habit. I would spend days awake trying to figure out what to do about everything, growing further from her. After 4-5 months she told me she was communicating with an EX she had cheated on me with. I exploded on her and she told me to end our relationship. 2 days later I was arrested for possession of SPILE & wound up at the Sanctuary, where I asked Jesus & the Holy spirit into my heart & July I was saved

Lucky To Be Alive

Testimony or Story: Well I Know I am here for a reason. As I was growing as a child I came from a Broken family I lived with my Mother, Grandmother and 3 sisters. My Mother. Father Divorced I was named after my Father. My Mother and GrandMother Hated My Dad he diden't pay Childsupurt So He wasent alowd to see us often. So me being the only Boy with the same name as my father worst end of Deal. So I Guess you could call me the Black sheep. So Fianily my Mother sent me to Live with my Dad and Grandfather witch were heavy Drinkers and it wasent easy either. well my Freshman year in highschool wasent good either so during summer Breack I got a Job on the Beach Painting high--rise Condminiens Thats is when the Drug's & Achoul played a majour part in my life I never went back to school Thats when the neardeath accidents started The First accidents was I Dove Through a window Lost over half my Blood On the way to the hospital I first Lost my vision then I Lost my hereing

(use back of sheet if needed)

Mail to :   Hellfighter
One Freedom Square
Laurel MS 39440-3367

But I still Knew what was going on I colasped at the
E.R Door thats all I rember, The next near death experiance
I was at the Club on the Beach about 30 guy's started
chaseing us down my friend said hit the water I went Tward
The water get in They started Throughing Big Limestone
rock's at us. one hit me in the head knocked me out
They said I was floating in the water nest thing I was
wakeing up in the hospital after haveing skull
fragments off my Brain. I recoverd went Back to work
in Luffkin Tx. I got ranover By a full size truck my
head was in Between The tire and the asphault
It Broke my rib's knocked out my teeth tore my ear
off eyes stiched up Broke nose had nose sugery
had to have False teeth should of Died well I
Recoverd once again went Back to work in Miami
got into a wreck on the Florda TurnPike was through
through The windshield Through 100 yards Ordent
even know what happend all I rember was
comeing to and I was crawling out of the ditch the
only engeny I had was a small cut on my head
took about Ten stiches, the other passanger had is
Back Broke and was paralised, came Back to Mobile
AL. where I grew up went to work got up one
morning headed to work on the Bayway it was very
Fogy got on the Bayway Bridge Before I had a chance
to hit the Breack's we ran into a pile of wrecked. It was
so foggy I knew that more car's were fixing to run into us
I got out of the truck there was a old laddy erying, please
make the car's stop about that time a Big Trash truck ran in
to my truck I started running Down the Bridge Flaging the
car's Down They couldent see what they were fixing to run
Into The car's started Locking up tires the car's were slideing
all around me I noticed that the cars were comeing to a stop I
stoped runing The next thing the cars started pileing up Behind
them for about 20 min. There were over 200 car pile up
with 15 cars in the middle with out a scrath Mobile Press Called
me a Hero That was not me that was GOD. Thank you

My Dad Was a Drunk

Hello,

My Name is ▓▓▓▓▓▓▓ I was born on ▓▓▓▓ in Cleveland, son of an auto mechanic slash DRUNK. Moved to ▓▓▓▓, Ms at age 4. My dad shot someone and went to prison. My mother had a nervous break down when I was 11 yrs old, I went to live with the oldest of 4 sisters. Needless to say I've had a bad childhood, always felt alone, no friends, I started drink'n and smoke'n pot at 13 yrs old At the age of 18 yrs til I was 25 yrs old I used every chance I got. My father died New Years Day of ▓▓ I got Married May of ▓▓ Had a son ▓▓ in August ▓▓▓▓▓ My drink'n got ▓▓▓ worse My Mother died ▓▓▓▓▓ then my drug use got worse. Moved to Tuscaloosa, Al in ▓▓, thinking I'd quit use'ing drugs, Well it got worse again. In Feb ▓▓ my youngest son was born, I thought I'd quit by now, but "crack" came into the picture. By the time ▓▓ rolled around I was divorced, Then everything went down hill, lost my job, lost what friends I had. It was just me ALONE, On May 12th I left Columbus ▓▓ on foot headed to Fla, Didn't make it, God stopped me in Thomasville Al, Where I stayed 6 wks at a Homeless shelter, I called my oldest sister and told her I needed more than A.A. + NA,

So, My next to oldest sister found a little ole place in ~~████████~~, Ms. ~~████████~~ since I came here ~~████~~, I've gotten what I needed to get on the right track. That is God!!! He works slow but he's kept me sober so far, I can tell a big difference in my life, My sisters & I don't fight, I'm not angry at the world, I have forgiven everything. I write my children, I can talk to my ex-wife with out getting angry.

I've only been here 12 days & I'm love'n it. It's a church camp for adults, I've been in & out of church all my life but didn't know how to live a christian life until now, and I've got alot still to learn.

God Bless All!!!

Mark 11:24

My Family Sucks!

My drug usuage has been out of control for a very long time now. I was raised in a church enviroment, but not in a spiritual one. In other words, we went to church every Sunday and prayed befor meals, but that was the extent of our religious practice. There was alway yelling and fighting between my parents. My Dad drank + comitted adultry. He hung out late nights in bars and would come home, start a fight with my mom, who never drank (just cursed heavily) which usually resulted in physical abuse. Because I hated the yelling more so than all other disfunctions our family had, I started running away at thirteen years old. They locked me up in a hospital for several months for runaway idiation (whatever that means). That was in the middle of my 12th grade. When I was released we moved

from GA to ████████ Befor I finished
school I had met what would
become my abusive husband. For
the next 4 years he would force
me to do drugs of all kinds and
phyically & mentally abuse me.
I had my daughter at 20 years
off & divorced him at 21 years old.
Alcohol was the choice of my self destruction for the first years of my
addition. In my 30's I started using
pain pill. Not just from one doctor, but
I ran as many as I could find. I
had an accident in ████ that caused me
to have two spinal surgeries. I had
convinced my self I needed these pills.
Because I liked the pills more than the
alcohol, I quit the alcohol so I could
take more pills. That lasted about 4
years. Then I believe God sent this
special man (angel) into my life who
demand quit the pills or I'm leaving —
well because this was the first time
I ever fell in love, I quit. But being
the addict I was inside, I secretly
switched to cocaine. It didn't matter

how I did it - crack (smoke), shoot or snort, I liked them all. Just the past few months - March - July, I died from overdose about 6 times. Medical people have said it was a miracle they were able to bring me back. If I added up all the times I've had guns to my head, attempted rapes, muggings, car wrecks, taking 100 pills and shooting up drugs + ~~that~~ yet God wont let me die, I realize now that he must have some special purpose for me and I refuse to let the devil get any more of the time God owns. He died for me + deserves all my time I have left or more. I thank him daily for not letting me go the way I was headed - to hell

God loves me.

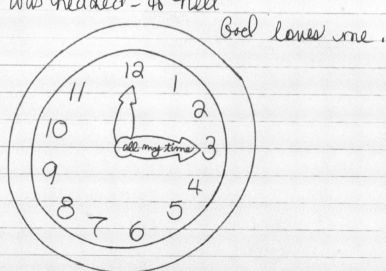

My Father Stole My Virginity

Dear Robert

My name is ▓▓▓▓▓▓▓▓▓▓
I was Born in a home that was
very caotic, my mom and dad was
always drunk or high It was a
party at my house all the time
I started getting abused at an
early age and that took me
on a emotional spiral to a
place that would be my home
for many years I started drinking
and drugging to be normal and
not feel the pain that I was
enduring my father beat us
all the time. Every time we
turned around my mother got
it the worse. ▓▓▓▓ I needed
more and more to fill that
void. I got pregant at 16
my mother was very sickly
and died the same year I
had my baby she left me
with my father that sexually
Abused and physically messed
my mind up for many more
years to come

I was old enough to
leave home but I would
get with men like my
father if you know what
I mean that kind of life was
familier to me the only
life I knew and I needed
more + more to fill that hurt
I was feeling I was
introduced to Christ later,
but wasnt serious until
the devil stole everything
I had; my family friends
children and my own life
I lost all self control
and I was ready to let
god in my life for the
first time I was ready
to let him control my
everything I was tried I
have a life today without
drugs or alcohol playing a
part in my life god is
slowly giving me back
my life that the devil
stole from me

never be Discouraged

There's is nothing we need to know or ever tryed to understand if we refuse to be discouraged and trust Gods guiding hand so take heart and meet each minute with faith in God's great love aware that every day of life is Controlled by God Above and never dread tommorrow Or what the future brings Just pray for strenght + Courage and trust god in all things and never be discouraged, be patient and Just wait for gods he never comes to early and never come's to late in god world he never make mistakes

Thanks

I need Prayer right now nothing else at this time

Ps this was the hardest thing I had to do thanks to god for his Grace + mercy in my life today

Thank you

My Husband Dumped Me

I got married right out of High school to a wonderful guy! During our marriage of 27 years, we had 2 great children. Our lives were very normal and had a fantastic marriage until the last year. He was working all the time in the Oil field and I worked in the Emergency room of a hospital. The last year of our marriage we seemed to drift apart for some reason. We were both very tired and worked such long hours, we just stopped trying I suppose. My husband's high school sweetheart - (just divorced for the third time) started calling my husband and showing up at places he attended. Long story short - He left me for her, and I was devastated. My mom died 8 months earlier, so I hadn't got over grieving for her, then I was getting a divorce.

My world fell apart:

I have never been in trouble in my life. (Not even a speeding ticket)

I started drinking to cover up the pain. I've never took any drugs, so that was not an option. In 9 months time I received 3 DUI's. I am at this recovery center to deal with my pain, so I will never get into any more trouble.

I realize how stupid I was to make those mistakes, but, at the time, my pain was unbearable.

I am doing this for me and my children. They need their mom back like she was, and they love me so much!

Thanks for listening to me!

My Kid's Mama is a Drug Addict

RH's Note: The Devil sure is good at what he does.

Testimony or Story: I grew up in a loving home with both parents. When I was 12 i started hanging out with a older crowd of People. Its was then i started smoking Pot And drinking. I had my first child at age 15 and my Second at 17. I met my husband, he smoked crack, cocain. I then formed a issue with it myself. I thought for awhile it was managabel. my life became very complicated. I made up reasons so i could use. Then i found Pills when i then discovered how to shoot up. I know have four children and their mother is a drug attick. my mother takes care of them. I feel horribel. Ive let everyone down. my babies are getting so big. they need their mother. Im hear now for myself, And my Loved ones. I wont to be that girl that did it. When People See me I wont them to be abel to Say, She did that. I wont a normal life. I wont my babies to have their mother and my mother to have the daughter She raised!

(use back of sheet if needed)

My Mom Married My Dad's Brother

When I was about 2 years old my mother and father divorsed. My mother was seeing my dads half-brother. My dad has been a drunk all his life. He works offshore so he has everything he wants. So I lived with my mama and stepdad. As a kid I can remember them allways smoking weed and partying, drinking, + fighting My parents didn't get along because of her leaving him for his brother. My dad always tried to pick a fight with anybody so it wasn't the best living conditions. I lived with my mom all through school. In High School I started smoking weed, drinking. But during High School my step-father hurt his-self working and got put on pills. He started abusing them. Then my mama took ahold of it. That went on for years. My senior year my mama got hooked on crack leavin me and my lil brother at home, no food, lights and water gettin cut off pretty regular. Step father stayed in bed raising hell. So I took it upon myself to quit school and take on a Full-time job and taking G.E.D Classes.

My mama kept on with her crack. So I went to look for her and found her one night cracked out at the waffle house with 2 flat-tires and she didn't know what happened so I called her daddy and told him and told him to come get her. He did and so I was on my own then. My dad was working offshore at the time so I worked and stayed on streets till he came home and I went and stayed with him. But he kicked me out on Fathers day of ████. I was 16. So from there it was all streets. From couch to couch. I kept on working and making money but all drugs sex and sin was in my life. I got me and apartment with my ████████ and thats where it really got bad. I met a girl that fliprd my world upside down. It staved with an Oxy. From there a little ice and then I broke my hand fighting and couldn't work and decided to start cooking my own dope. To make money which I started smoking too. Then I lost apartment, job, & my 'CAR'. Thats when I thought I had to

Steal to make it. I started out at Wall-mart + dollar stores then it went to big bussiness, houses. Whatever it took it keep me goin wit a sack of weed and to shake up some more dope. and sex. But the stealing got bad as to kickin in doors and taking everything to robbin the dope-man I eventually got caught up stealin Rims and a as hard as it is to say this I robbed my own grand-Father for a flat-screen T.V. and a safe I went to prison for it. Got 5 years Did 1-year and rest on paper. Prison tault me alot but I didn't seek god at that time. Just a bunch of gang-bangers tryin to run a prison. I got out and did good for a year, But found myself slipping back into take same things that got me where I was. I wanted help but wasn't willing to help myself to one day was getting high and that the last I remember I woke up with my girl-Friend over me beating me sayin you can't die. I had blood all over me, didn't know what happened

But she said I was dead for
about 3 min. And that really opened
my eyes and told myself I got to
get help. But I didn't wanna leave
her or the streets. But I knew, if
I didn't I would soon be in a
box or in a cell. So I found
the Hell-Fighters through a woman
that works with my mama at
████████████████████ She saw me comin
to ^where my mama works ██████████) always
lookin ruff. Beggin for money or to
get somethin to eat. And she told
me about this place. and know I had
been living on river for a few months
and I didn't have my mind set
on it. I told her to give me that
last weekend out and I know I was
comin here but was scared and didn't
know what to do. So that last
weekend It rained mostly so I sat
in tent just cryin and beggin god
to show me the way. So I did. I
let everything go and surrender
everything and laid it in gods hands.
Laid on my problems at the alter.
Since I have been here he has

givin me a clear head and a loving heart Not like the cold harted selfish person I was. ▆▆

▆▆▆▆▆▆▆▆▆▆▆▆▆▆▆▆▆▆▆▆
▆▆▆▆▆▆▆▆▆▆▆▆▆▆▆▆▆▆▆▆
▆▆▆▆▆▆▆▆▆▆▆▆▆▆▆▆▆▆▆▆
▆▆▆▆▆▆▆▆▆▆▆▆▆▆▆▆▆▆▆▆
▆▆▆▆▆▆▆▆▆▆▆▆▆▆▆▆▆▆▆▆
▆▆▆▆▆▆▆▆▆▆▆▆▆▆▆▆▆▆▆▆

I still worry alot About things but I remind myself to "Take my Paws off of it and put it in gods hands and he will take care of it."

My Mom Was a Lesbian

Dear Hellfighters,

I used to hate God and blame him for all things wrong in my life. Being born to a lesbian mother I was robbed of a father and a normal childhood. This in my eyes made me a misfit. I know what it meant to have something missing at an early age. I went to chatholic school from first to fourth grade so I was introduced to god early in life. I was happy for a while, then I was taken out of private school and put into public school, it was a shock to my young spiritual being. I hated public school. I went from being cool or normal to outsider or misfit. <u>GOD WAS TAKEN OUT OF MY SCHOOLING</u> so the things I had stop worrine about came back with vengence. About that time I was molested by older cousins every weekend.

THE SEED OF HATRED WAS SOWN AND
I WOULD QUESTION GOD WHY ARE
THESE THING HAPPENING TO ME? WHAT
DID I DO TO DESERVE SUCH A HARD
LIFE? I GAVE UP ON GOD FOR I
FELT SURELY HE HAD GIVEN UP ON
ME. I BEGAN SMOKING AND DRINKING
BY TIME OF THE 6th GRADE.
I SPENT THREE YEARS IN THE
6th GRADE. 6, 6, 6, mmmm SOUND
FORMILIAR. I BECAME A THEIF AND
A LIAR. I BEGAN PUTTING MY FAITH
IN THE SATANIC BIBLE. MY HEART
BECAME AS PITCH AND I SENT
FORTH THE DARKNESS TO DO MY
BIDDING. KIDS THAT USED TO
PICK ON ME NOW FEARED ME
OR WANTED TO BE LIKE ME.
I MADE A DEAL WITH THE
DEVIL TO NO LONGER BE THE
VICTIM OF A SO CALLED LOVING
GOD. IN RETURN FOR BRINGING
HIM FOLLOWERS I COULD

HAVE ANYTHING I DESIRED.
I HAD A HEDGE OF WICKEDNESS
SURROUNDING ME. BAD THINGS
WOULD HAPPEN 2 THOSE WHO HATED ME
BECAUSE AFTER ALL HATE BELONGS
TO THE DARK ONE. ONE OF THE
COUSINS WHO MOLESTED ME AS A
CHILD HAS BEEN SUFFERING WITH
HIV FOR OVER 15 YEARS NOW. I
REMEMBER IT ALWAYS COMING IN
TO SIGHT OR HEARING THAT THOSE
WHO HURT OR WRONGED ME ANSWERED
FOR IT. THIS MADE MY FAITH
IN DARKNESS GREATER. EVEN
IN THE FACE OF THIS DARK SECRET
I FELT ALONE. I WAS STRAPING
MORE AND MORE BONDAGE UPON MY-
SELF. I BEGAN TO FEEL GUILTY.
I HAD SO MUCH HATE AND UN-
FORGIVENESS IN ME, I FORGOT
HOW TO LOVE. I HAD NO RESPECT
FOR WOMEN. THEY WERE NO THING
BUT SEX OBJECTS TO ME. MY

DEAL WITH SATAN WHERE GIRLS
WERE CONSERNED WAS THIS. I WAS
GIVEN THE HOLLYWOOD CHARM OF
DRACULA. THEY WERE PUPPETS
ON MY STINGS. I TURNED
CHRISTIAN GIRLS INTO HEATHEN SLUTS
BY THE DOZENS. THE MORE MENTALLY
I SPIT ON AND BEAT THEM THE MORE OBEIDIANT
THEY BECAME. I HAD DOZENS OF
HEARTS IN SLAVERY TO ME. BUT
IF I FELL IN LOVE ONE OF THESE
GIRLS THEY TURNED AGAINST ME AND
HATE ME. SO LUST BECAME
THE ONLY LOVE I KNEW WHEN
I WAS IN DARKNESS. LOOKING
BACK NOW I KNOW I DIDN'T DESERVE
LOVE, BUT STILL SOME WHERE DEEP
INSIDE ME, I SCREAMED FOR LOVE.
UNABLE TO FILL THE HOLE IN MY
HEART I TURNED TO DRUGS.
I WAS DEPESSED TO THE POINT
OF SUISIDE. IN FACT, MANY TIMES
I TRIED TO OVER DOSE.

THE SAME DRUGS I USE TO
INSLAVE WOMEN ENSLAVED ME!
MY LUST FOR SHOOTING COCAINE
BECAME GREATER EVEN THAN FOR
SEX. MY DESTINATION TO HELL
SPEEDING CLOSER AND CLOSER.
MY GUILT FOR MY SINS OVER WELMING
ME. MY SELF HATE ENORMUS. I
FELT THAT I DESERVED HELL FOR
ETERNITY. I WAS READY FOR MY
SENTENCE. CLOSE TO DEATH,

    GODS INTERVENTION CAME TO
ME BY WAY OF A LOCAL OUTREACH
MINISTRY CALLED GROUND ZERO. I
WAS WORKING AT A TATTOO PARLOR
AROUND THE CORNER FROM THE MINISTRY.
A LONG TIME COMRADE IN DARKNESS,
WHO WORKED WITH ME BEGAN TO
HANG OUT WITH THE GUY'S FROM
THE MINISTRY. I WATCH SOMEONE
WHO WOULD SPIT ON CHRISTIANS AT
THE MENTION OF JESUS SLOWLY
BE TRANSFORMED. I WATCHED

A PAGAN BECOME A CHRISTIAN.
I WITNESSED A MIRACLE BEFORE MY EYES.
I WENT TO A FEW BIBLE STUDIES
WITH THESE GUYS. I NOTICED THE
JOY AND HAPPINESS THAT THEY HAD
THROUGH JESUS. I BEGAN TO SEE
WITH AMAZEMENT THAT JESUS
WAS THE ANSWER. I REALIZE
THAT HE WAS THE ONLY FILLER
FOR THE WHOLE IN MY HEART.
THE DEVIL HAD ME SO BLIND TO
FACT THAT IT WAS HIS HAND
THAT MADE MY LIFE SO MISERABLE.
I BECAME WHAT I SHOULD HAVE
HATED MOST. I FELT SO ASHAMED
OF MYSELF. SO UNWORTHY OF HIS
LOVE. BUT HE REJOYCED AND SAID
HE LOVED ME STILL BECAUSE HE
NEVER GAVE UP ON ME, HIS LITTLE
LOST LAMB. ALL THE PAIN OF
32 YEARS OF PICTH BLACK
DARKNESS HAS BEEN BLEACHED
BY THY LOVING LIGHT OF CHRIST.

I FEEL LIKE A NEW BORN. I FEEL LIKE I NEVER even KNEW JOY til NOW. GOD'S GRACE is so AMAZING to ME. JESUS Died for ME AND ALL I WANT TO DO IS WORSHIP HIM FOREVER. I WANT TO LOVE HIM FOREVER AND EVER. I DESERVE TO DIE A HORRIBLE DEATH. BUT HE DiED THAT HORRIBLE DEATH FOR ME. I BELIEVE IN HIM AND ALL OF HIS GLORY. FROM NOW ON, IF MY LIFE DOESN'T GLORIFY HIM WHO LOVES US, I'D RATHER BE DEAD. I WANT JESUS TO KNOW THAT FOR HIM I WOULD MOST SURELY BE A

Hell fighter!

Yours Truly,

My Paychecks Just Disappeared

My Testimony

I'm a 38 year old man currently staying at the a rehab facility for Men. Today is Sun. July ███████, and I just finished reading my Bible. Every-day I think about how my life would be without Jesus. I can't believe I went so long without my best friend (Jesus Christ).

It all started when I was 15 years old. I was introduced to marijuana back in my home town of ████████████ ███. A classmate from Catholic school asked me one day if I would like to try smoking a joint. At the time I had been skipping out of Church and growing farther away from my religious faith. So I tried it and fell in love with the feeling. I would go from smoking one joint about every 3 days, to 1 joint everyday in less than 1 month. And as everyone knows, that got old and I was on the search for a different high.

By the age of 17, I started drinking alcohol. I would never do it before school, but as soon as 3:00 PM arrived, we were out of school and behind the levee smoking weed and getting drunk.

It took about 3 years of doing that before my parents caught on. I would constantly deny their accusations for fear of being sent away to treatment. As all of this was going on, I quit going to church, I stopped praying and I also stopped saying my Rosary. I always knew that losing my faith in God would catch up to me one day.

I was now 20 yrs. old and a friend introduced me to cocaine. That's when my life really started to spiral down hill. I would get job after job and would always get fired from them because I hated to get up in the morning for work, so I missed alot. And every job I would get, the paychecks would be gone on that day I received them.

By the age of 25, I started smoking Crack because my nose would bleed everytime I snorted a line. When I took that first hit of crack, something inside of me told me I would die. Well I was right, I died to all family members and friends. I didn't want anyone around me and, not even talk to people.

Then, when I was 27 I went into a bar one night and met this girl I grew up with from my home-town. We started dating and eventually got married. One year later she gave me my own angel. A beautiful red haired Daughter (I have red hair) and when she was 6 months old I went get a vasectomy because I knew I wouldn't be able to share my love with another child. During all of this I actually quit doing everything, even the cigarettes.

Then one day I found out my wife (exwife now) Cheated ## on me.

I was devastated so I left her with the house, car and all the bills. And yes I went back to all the drugs.

Finally, 8 years later I was spending time with my daughter when she asked me a question that floored me. She asked me if I was doing drugs. Well, one week later I was here at the recovery center I put myself in here because I was meant to do greater things: serve the Lord, to be a soldier for Christ and be the father to my now 9 yr. old beautiful baby girl, I new I could be.

I'm starting phase 2 tomorrow which means I have 6 weeks left in here. My daughter writes me letters telling me that she's so proud of me & even my family is proud of me. My ex-wife is my best friend and I'm doing great in my recovery because I don't put my Bible down, I live by the Word because I know that the battle will never end.

I know that I will do good when I get out because I notice that sometimes I'm the only one getting up a 5:00 AM, going to the Chapel and praying. Even during the day, I constantly have my Bible with me and I'm always reading it and following the Word. My counselor says I'm the maturest one in my group and he says he can tell I'm hungry for this.

I got saved on June 14th, ██████ in here at the recovery center for men and on Aug. ██ 2nd, ████ I graduate from here and my work begins. My goal is to show my daughter how wonderful life is in Jesus Christ. She already sees how much I've changed and she's asking a lot of religious questions.

I now love life and my Savior Jesus Christ because through Him all things are possible. I'm living proof of that.

Will you please send me a Big Bible and a Shirt because I admire

what the Hell Fighters are about and
the Bible I saw from some of the
guys in here are beautiful ▓▓▓▓
▓▓▓▓▓▓▓▓▓▓▓▓▓▓
    Thank you for your time and your
prayers.
                Your Brother & Friend,

My Son's Mom Still Loves Me

Greetings In the name of our Lord + Savior Jesus Christ.

Let me begin with expressing an appology for not putting the proper amount of Info in the "topics" regarding My Testimony. I'm sorry!

Now, Let me tell you, I feel overwhelmed in getting this request! I'm quite certain you get a large amount to read probably daily, and to be interested in more about my past (drugs, alcohol + prison) But I do indeed hope + pray this will Bless you and you will prise Him with me! For He is Certainly worth it!!

It's been about 20 yrs. ago when God started to draw me to Himself (I'll spare you the wonderful details regarding that). but I used cocaine + drank vodka. I was 22 years old, I had a good Job that paid very well. I didn't know that the girlfriend I had (   ) had been raised a christian (but had backslidden) The cocaine + Alcohol continued to get worse + worse, which led   to start to pray again but I didn't know it. then one day   came to me a said "   , I'm pregnant!" I thought she was only trying to "get her hooks in me, so I told her to get an abortion" then the Lord over drew me closer again + I Met a ⤷

Pastor Paul ████████████ and I
had asked to talk to him
about all my problems. Once I
told him about my girlfriend &
the abortion we were going to get
he asked me to come to his house
that night with ██████ & we could
speak to him & his wife.
   When ██████ got home from work
that day and was in the middle
of cooking dinner I said to her
"   " when she looked at me
I said "Let's get with God." I
was startled at the way she broke
out crying. (I didn't understand) we
went to the pastors house that night
and she recommitted her life to
God and I accepted Jesus as
my savior. Oh how I'd love to
be able to tell you "And we lived
happily ever after." But oh NO
little did I know about the
spiritual battle that had begun
in my life. The pastor who led me
to the Lord knew deeper "disciple-
ship was needed." I enrolled in Teen
Challenge" (after a few different
states (Maryland, Boston, Fla. Penn.) I
finally completed 1 year. This had
already begun to leave ████████ with
the responsibility of raising a child
(████████████) but she held on
(believing God would work things out.) →

248

After completing Teen Challenge I
was asked by the Director of the
Center where I went through "Induction"
"What do you want to do?" I was
confused. He helped me in finding my
options which was going to College
If I chose. I filled out the
application for a Bible College +
Student loans and was amazed
(stuned!) ████████ was not impressed
when I informed her that I could go
to College In florida. (we lived in
Maryland). She tried to talk me out of
it and I simply told her "don't make
me choose between you or college" (I
thought school was what God wanted.)
I had told her I would go the
first semester and once I got used
to school, then I would bring her ███
████████ down + we would get married.
While going to School I surrounded
myself with people who were serious about
the Lord + school. I chose a church
that was well grounded. But you see
████████, they were not aware of
the sins in my life (abandoning ████████
+ our son ████████) I even made it
look good and to Cover the guilt
I was experiencing I volunteered
to drive the van to pick up Kids.
I got involved with a woman
I went to school with and I over
didn't even consider the sin G

that was controling my life.
Well "summer break" came +
all my "spiritual friends" went
back to whatever state they had
came from. So this left me right
there. eventually my attendance
at church slacked. eventually
I came to believe that drinking
only 1 beer wouldn't hurt. well
once I accepted this thought
it changed to hey if that's the
case, why not just go to the
"club" right up the street?
well that's what I did, and
as far as that "1 that wouldn't
hurt", I spent $400.00 that night
on crack cocaine. it was
"all out" from there within 1
months time I was arrested 3
times for possession and ~~would~~
wound up being sent to Prison.
▓▓▓▓▓▓, this was the 1st time,
after that I was called to N.J. to
work. there's alot of ugliness
involved. But there is two people
who wouldn't "give up" on me
The Lord Jesus Christ And
My son's Mom ▓▓▓▓. I wound
up having to serve 6 years
on a 7 year sentence in Jersey.
But I had contacted ▓▓▓▓
whenever the other (non-believing)→

women I knew "went there own way" after my "time" was done in Jersey, the woman I was involved with from ▮ had moved to ▮▮▮▮,

I thought I had learned My lesson + would be able to live a "good life" from then on out. But there was 1 thing missing, and I could Not live without it! I didn't have Jesus christ in my daily living, I was living in Sin. So after only 2½ Months after doing 6 years I wound up back in prison (for drinking + crack cocaine).

I began to get my life back in order to serve the Lord, I repented and began to study + pray daily. I began to think + pray for my son ▮▮▮▮ sr and his Mom ▮▮▮▮▮ I prayed that we could be a family to love + serve God. Well that night when they were giving out Mail they called My Name.

It was a post card from ▮▮▮▮! She was worried about me after Katrina and she got on the Computer to see if I might be dead. Next she checked the Hospitals. She knew next to check police stations she got in touch with a chaplain who gave her my address. we've been growing closer + closer back to where God wants for us to Be. But we're Certainly taking everything In God's timing + not our own Go over

████ has faithfully + patiently waited for God to perform the work that is taking place we will have a whole lott of work to do concerning our son Michael Jr. (who just turned 20 yrs. old + I'm sure is quite bitter + need God's love + power in his life.)

Bro. Hell Fighter Robert

I do indeed hope this has been a blessing to you. I realize I am not worthy of two things I've already been given.

1) the gift of my salvation +
2) the committed love of a woman who was so terribly treated.

One thing that I've set forth is to be all that she has expected, waited + prayed for for 20 yrs.

I would be willing to give her the Bible + T-shirt that I've been offered; but I would be greatly appreciative if her + I were able to receive A Matching set. (when we set out in our spiritual warfare of whitnessing + teaching, we would be very proud to proclaim we are indeed called to be in the Hell fighters "A League of extraordinary Ladies + Gentlemen" May God Strength + Blessing continue to surround + fill you! your Brother in christ

Now I'm a Hellfighter!

_HICKS

I am a Prisoner in the ████████ State
Prison - Main Unit, and
I have been incarcerated since ████.

       a life of crime, in which led me
to this 25 year prison sentence for D.U.I
Manslaughter and two bodily injury's...
Sin cost me everything I love, my family
Friedom and Friends... I rode with one
of the most notorious Biker Gangs in the
United States of America, and THOUGHT
I was the coolest thing since peanut butter
but little did I know that I was ~~headed~~
a to Hell Bound sinner in need of a Savior.
In ████ I got busted in Yakima Washington.
State for a small crime, and while in jail
a true HellFighter came to my rescue, and
led me to the Cross of Christ Jesus, were
I went from a sinner to a saint in
Christ Jesus our Lord... I repented of
everything I ever done and received
Christ Jesus as my Lord and Savior.
As a New Born Babe in Christ, I was
Never Discipled, and shortly after I was
released I backslid into the old biker
life style, which was grieving the
Holy Spirit inside me, but I did not

understand why, because no one took the time to disciple me... then like I said at the begging of this testimony, I got into some big trouble in which cost somebody their life and me my freedom in 1998... Once Again sin took me farther than I wanted to go and has keept me longer than I wanted to stay... Sin may have cost me a lot in this physical world, but in the spiritual I have been set free in Christ Jesus our Lord... My body may be in Prison but our Lord and Savior has set me free (John 8:32;36) I have rededicated my life back to Christ Jesus for God and will never turn back again. I have earned my Masters Degree in the Ministry and plan on earning a D.R. Degree Next. I have Ministered to all of Death Row and Close Management 1 2 and 3 inmates as well as open population inmates. I have helped lead several people to Christ Jesus, and have passed out hundreds of HellFighter tracts as well as other tracts, and I fill that I am Qualified to be a true HellFighter and would love to be a Part of Your Ministry. I would be honored to be a Patch holder Hellfighter... Is this possible for a man like me, with a 25 year sentence? I hope to hear the answer to that question soon... May God continue to Bless all of the true Hellfighters in Christ Jesus... Amen

In Jesus Service,

Old Soldiers Do Drugs Too

Hi! Robert Smith   I'M ~~███████████~~
       This is my Testimony I AM 42 yrs of age

<u>I started Drinking at the age of 9.</u> My Mother
started letting me have a beer when we would
go fishing. That led to me steeling beer from
her and her friends. <u>by the age of 12 i was
smoking Pot and doing Acid (LSD).</u> By the age
of 15 i had Quit school and started doing Cocaine.
And selling pot had a 27 yr Old girl friend.
Then when i thought i had it made! life hit
me hard at 16 my father was arrested and sent
to prison for Child Molesting. I was left Homeless
and no money a lesbian Mother that didn't care
if i even lived. I turned to my Grandparents
who were Devout Pentecostal Christians.
they took me in and probably at the time
saved my life. or saved me from prison.
they helped me until I Got a Job and was able to
support myself. Then as soon as I was going to
move out My Grandmother died. My Grandfather
took it so hard he had to move in with my
aunt. so here I was homeless again.
so i went back to selling drug's!
at the age of 24 went in USMC
(united States Marine Corps) served 8yrs. Did not make
me a man still. I thought i was But i wasn't.
well i signed Back up for 8 more in special OPS

within a year was accepted into Black OPS
specia forces. Became a sniper went too 17
different Countries killed in 13 of them.
Done things you could not imagine. was a paid
assasin for the USA in my mind. commited murder
more than 340 times but was ordered to do so.
did one tour 18mos in Bosnia - 18mos in Afganistan -
- 18mos in Iraq - another 4mos in Iraq Got Blew up
By IED road side bomb outside of Anbar Provence. My best
friend my spotter of 6yrs was killed also 2 other men.
in a hummer. I was driving Big Dave my spotter was sitting
to my right. It blew him all over me his tib bone out
of his right leg stuck in my Jaw - broke my Jaw in 4 places.
almost blew my rt foot off my Rt arm Below my elbow but
they put it Back on. Broke Pelvis in 6 Placest Both hips.
Broke 7 ribs Punctured lung torn splein. Severe head injury.
4 Drain tubes in my head. lost all my memory for 11mos -
started getting it Back. almost got all of it Back now
still don't remember a lot of my life with my wife.
but she is a devout Christian and Has stood by me
100 %. ▓▓▓▓▓▓▓▓ was told i would never walk again
after 2 Hips. 3 plates in rt leg im walking.
very Good. and getting stronger. But Became a severe
Alcoholic Drug Addic. Now im at the mission ▓▓▓▓
and see the light at the end of the tunnel.
I Am A new man Have Bee Cleansed by the blood
of christ. / I want to see about helping in

spreading the word with a group your group
I'm retired with a pretty good pension.
I served the Devil long enough now its time to
serve Christ. would you write me back i
would love to become a soldier. can't ride
a bike but can drive. one day I'll be able
to ride again. But that doesn't matter to me
what matters is serving the lord.

    Sincerely ████████████

    Retired = Master Sargent

    (USMC)   (Gunny)

One Day at a Time

My life has truly been a roller coaster.
I was raised in a good christian home to say the least.
My mother was a good christian woman who worked
her but off to make sure I had everything I wanted &
needed. My mother & father got divorced when I was
a baby, he was a heavy alcoholic. I didnt really know
my father until I turned 13 & My mother sent me to
stay with him because I was giving her so much trouble.
She had my little brother to take care of though, so I
dont blame her I was a hand full. When I was
12 my mother had been remarried for a few years & had
my brother. It seemed like everything was peaches & cream,
because I was a kid & didnt have a trouble in the world
to my knowledge. I was raised in church, was in the youth.
Mother made sure we were all in church every Sunday &
in youth on wednesday. My brothers dad was having
problems with our mother, but I didnt know I was only
a kid. He started drinking heavy & mother & him were
in the process of building a house at big horn lake. We
were renting a place waiting on the house to get built.
One night I'll never forget, Jay: pulled in late & mother
told me to g stay inside because we were watching a
movie, it was the Post man with Kevin costner. I stayed
on the couch while she walked outside.

I'll never forget what happened next. I was
looking through the window + mother meet Jay, at the
steps of the front porch. They were arguing + then
Jay hit her in the face + then he walked inside
the house. He walked right past me + from the look
in his eyes I could tell something was very wrong with
him. My brother was in the back room asleep where
Jay was heading. I ran outside to see my mother + she
was in the car calling the police. She told me to go + hide
in the woods, but I didnt I followed her to the window where
Jay was at in the room. We saw him in the closet loading
his 223 rifle. My little brother was asleep in the same
room where he, was loading the rifle. Mother told me
no matter what happens not to come inside that she had
to go get my brother outa the house. I was so scared
+ confused you could only imagine the things going through my
mind as a kid. She went inside + the feelings of helplessness
drownded me to where I was sick to my stomach. All I heard
was loud comossion + things being nocked over + yelling. It
seemed like forever + then she came running out coverd in blood
with MY BROTHER in her arms. We all ran to the wood line + then
the cops showed up. She faught over the gun with Jay +
took it from him + busted his head with it. When the cops
got Jay + took him in the cop car I went inside

the house + their was blood everywhere. It looked like a truck had drove straight through the house it was a wreck. They got divorced + life went on. When I hit high school I started hanging out with the wrong crowd + really getting into trouble. mother did all she could do, so she sent me to live with my dad. I was 14 + I hated my dad, he was a drunk + treated me like crap. we had a big blow out + I went back to live a mothers. months passed by + I got home from school that day + mother told me that my dad was found dead in his front yard. I found out later he died from alcohol posin. 2 years pas + I was still hanging with the wrong crowd + I knew better because my mother has been in law enforcement long before I was born, I was raised better. I was hanging with older people doing drugs + getting kicked out of different schools. I was sent to rehabs + other stuff, nothing worked though. Mother spent so much money on me for different rehabs + help. I eventualy got kicked out the house + moved in with older friends. Things went from bad to ~~worse~~ worse. I eventualy got into trouble with the law + had to go to the rid program, I remember going before the judge scared to death.

I completed the rid program & went back home to mothers. I started working offshore & everything was good. I was 18 & rolling in the money. I meet some wild girls while home for my 2 weeks off. I started useing agian & moved outa the house the whole time mother pleding & praying for me not to that I was going to mess up agian. I was on probation & had to report monthly. I kept my job offshore for a year & still useing drugs heavy. The wild girls stayed around all the time not because of my good looks, but because of the money. I was driving to the docks for work snorting powder the whole way there. When I got there the tool pusher said they were doing random urine test. I knew I would fail & didnt want to piss, they caught me off guard. I had to pee though or I would lose my job so I did hoping they wouldnt test my urine sample. 3 days later on the rig they called me to the tool pushers office & the doctor was on the other end of the phone to tell me what I already knew. they fired me & sent me home on the next boat in. I got back to my truck & scared because I didnt want my probation officer to know & go back to prison, so I went on the run & stayed with those wild girls. 4 months later outa money & the woman gone I showed up at my grandmothers & the cops arrested me there. I ended up going to prison for long term A&D & ended up doing a year & 1/2. I got out on house arresst living at my mothers. It didnt take long for those old friends & habits to find me. I completed 16 months on house arresst & 2 months. into probation faund myself without a place to live & a warrent out for my arresst. My mother talked the P.O. & judge into sending me to Christian Recovery ctr. I completed 18 months & learned a lot. I was on fire for God & doing good, well great. I meet a wild women & slowly got outa church & back into drugs away from the Lord & everything I knew was pure & right. Im here at hell fighters now because God has so much more for me than Pain & suffering. I love Jeremiah 29:11. I know me being here is in his will, all I can do is trust in the lord & take it one day at a time.

Our Marriage Was Alcohol-based

Hi,

I am ████████ from ████ Mississippi. I arrived here at this Christian Recovery Center on March 23, ████. My arrival was by the Grace of God.

I am 55 years old and after 28 years of marriage, my husband left me for a woman 15 years younger than him and 10 years younger than me. I met my husband when I was seventeen and married at the age of 27. Our marriage was alcohol based from the beginning. We functioned — meaning we both worked and raised a daughter who is a Registered Nurse and will not touch Alcohol.

After she left home in ████, my world more or less fell apart. We also lost my husband's parents within three years of each other. All the above took place all around the same time.

We each sunk our sorrows in Alcohol and grew apart.

My marriage was a nightmare. We fussed, fought, had knock-down drag outs and toward the end of the marriage (10 months Ago)

The law was constantly being called by either me on him or him on me. I finally went to jail on January 1, with my second DUI. I sat in jail 6 weeks because no one would get me out. A lady named Wanda ministered to the female inn-mates at the ████ Co Denتورsion Center. I knew when I was locked up and heard that door slam shut and lock behind me that GOD had stepped into my life. I have known God all my life and has had a close relationship with him. My Problem was I would never hand it ALL to GOD. I wanted him in my life but I wanted to run the show. The six weeks I sat in jail I saw and experienced so many miraculous signs from God to let me know that he was with me. When GOD finally opened that jail Door and let me out, my new friend Wanda was there to take me home. She handed me a pamplet on ████ and after all my Court Appearances were complete and over, I was driven down to the Rehab Center by my Ex-husband and he is paying for my stay here.

He has stopped drinking but does not yet have his life on course with God.

Going to jail was the best thing that could have happened to me and Now I have the chance to devote three whole months to just walking and talking with GOD. I'm letting him run the show now and have No desire to take the reins back. What a mess I made!

Thank You for Being There,

Out of Control Since I was 13

Dear, Hellfighter's

My name is Richard
and I am at the ▓▓▓▓▓▓▓▓▓▓
I am 31 years old and I've
been on drugs and liquor since
the age of 13 years old. I've been
in and out of prison all my life.
I am struggling with my walk
with the Lord. Drugs have been
my life and I am trying to
live ~~coming~~ a good Christan walk
I came to the ▓▓▓▓▓ because this
last year I starting back on
drugs (pills) very bad. And got
arrested for pills.

I would love very much
to have one of those Bible
and T-shirts yall send to
the guys over here. My
shirt size is XL. Thank
yall so much and God Bless
yall.

God bless;

Prison is Tough

RH's Note:
Many people have no idea what goes on inside prison walls. Joe, a good friend of mine, agreed to tell you a little about Hell on earth.

Dear Richard & Gina,

Greetings and God Bless! I received your letter, Envelopes, paper and stamps and I thank both of you as always for your Kindness. Yes I did receive your photos in and of the new bike shop, The shop looks terrific and I hope all goes Well. Richard remember you Can ask me Any thing at all one thing I am is I am loyal and honest to friends. The reason Im back in the hole is because I was set up by black inmates Cause they claim Im a white supremacist and a leader of the Aryan Brotherhood, so these animals placed a Knife under the fold of my sheet on my bed and than sent the officers to my Cell to search while I was at the library. This is the type of things that are going on in prison, The Conditions hear are terrible and inhuman but it appears no one here Cares. I do agree that white folks are the minority we most Certainly are in this Jungle I am living in. So when they packed my property to be taken to Confinment they found some gang paraphernalia so I received 3 disciplinary Reports for Weapons and Gang stuff, I was found guilty at a Kangaroo hearing given 150 days and a referral to be Placed in a maxim Security lock down once again, I am waiting on a hearing for that, I will Keep you informed of my situation. There are numerous racial issues here and throuout the prison systems, I personally have been in Race Riots with all of the mongoloid Races at one time or another using Knives, pipes, locks, rocks in sox and at the end of some of these Confrontations somebody is needed to be medi-flighted out, Nearly always someone has to go to medical, Richard I Carry my scars and badges of these Battles, I know death is a Very Real possibility and I detest I am force to live this way to survive in this place, the years in prison I have walked over dead

bodies and Ive had guts splattered allover my chest from Race Wars. Might is right in this savage World I am forced to live in behind these gulag wires. I usually dont speak of these things but this is the way it truly is in prisons accross the U.S. ~~————————————————————~~ ~~————————————————————~~ ~~————————————————————~~ ~~————————————~~ yes you are right We will most likely be gone and not see the Race Wars in the streets, Ive seen enough stuff in here to last a life time. I am glad to hear the bike shop is doing great and your having a fund raiser to assist someone. I am also glad to hear buissness is good, I cannot have a hard back book in the situation Im in, But you can remove the hard Cover and send it with a note attached, Religious hard back Cover removed from publisher and I will recive it also remember to send me churchs under Religious also. I am Very glad to hear you and gina are doing great. ~~————————————————~~ ~~——————————————————————~~ ~~————~~ Well as far as my self I am doing well under the Circumstances, I feel healthy and my attitude is great. no matter what they do I remain Strong because only the strong will will survive here in this hell Im living in Well Richard & gina I close for now until I hear from you again Take Care & stay Strong and well

Your Friend

Puked to Death ___

My name is Julie ~~the rest is crossed out~~
~~of~~ I would like to give you my testimony, so that I may
recieve a bible. I really need one right now & it would help me
out alot. Thank you.

My Testimony:

The reason I am at this Rehab facility right now is
because my boyfriend and I made some extremely stupid
choices in March ~~8~~ of this year. We both did drugs, but
never considered ourselves addicts (like everyone does). He was
out a couple nights before, getting some marajuana and one
of our friends just gave him a free methadone wafer. a
couple days later he decided to take it (this was his
first time ever trying it), he also took zanbars w/ it and
about 30 min. later we decided to go to sleep. When he took it
he told me he only took half & I was even about to check to
make sure, but I believed him & let it go. The next morning
I woke up to get ready for work & went back in the room
to put my shoes on and to give him a kiss before I left.
(we were living at his parents house) as I got up to kiss
him I noticed he had his hands up to his chest, laying on
his side & he was face down in puke. I could tell that he
was dead. I was stunned, overwhelmed, in complete denial.
I went to the front room to tell his mom (I couldn't go to work
b/c there was something wrong with ~~him~~ (bf) and she could
tell something was wrong. I sat down on the sofa & immediately
started crying just to be brought to hysterics because his mom
was now shouting to me "Julie!! Julie he's dead!! ~~xxxx~~
~~xxxx~~" I couldn't say anything or do anything but sit there
and cry. he died on our ~~xxx~~ annivery day ~~xxxxxx~~ not
too long after that the police where there & I was brought

to be questioned. After about 4/5 hrs. of questioning I was brought to jail where I stayed for 2 wks & 4 days. That was my first time ever going to jail. I was extremely suicidal & didn't have any hopes for the future. One day in there a public defender asked me if I'd like to go to a christian Recovery center for emotional support & I gladly said yes. When I did get out of jail I got to go home for 2 weeks and in that time I got to go to ~~his~~ grave twice. I was really greatful for that & it helped me just to be able to sit and talk to him even though he was no longer with me now. ~~I'm at~~ this christian place ~~and it's taking me a little while, but I'm getting used to it.~~ I Don't really believe in god, but I think the concept is good & I could really use a bible of my own, so I can look at it in my free time. I would really ~~appreciate it~~ & thank you for reading my testimony.

Sincerely
Julie ████

RH's Note:
Julie's searching and if she won't give up, she will find the One who can fix her up.

"Ye shall find Me when you search for Me with all your heart."
- Jesus

Rehab + Jesus = Success

Hello. My name is ████. I've been at this Recovery Facility for Women for 14 days. I am in there because I am an alcoholic. My doctor said that if I didn't stop now, I will be dead in a few months. I have been in and out of the hospital four times since October. My family was with me at that visit. I became emotional and said to everyone that I was only 42 and too young to die. My sister attends Celebration Church in ████████ and talked to the pastor about me. Through their church, she hooked me up with a Christian Recovery Facility When I arrived I had to detox from alcohol and pain killers my doctor was giving me to help with the pain of my liver which was only operating at 10% capacity. I was taking Vicadin, Codiene, Dilandin, Hydrocodone and Morphine(sp), all on top of my alcohol that I continued to drink. I arrived and thought I was the worse person on the planet and I not only didn't deserve to be at this Recovery Facility but I didn't deserve to live. After only two weeks I realized that I wasn't alone. The counselors and the girls embraced me and made me feel like they are my sisters in Christ. Now, I can't wait to get to class, I can't wait to attend daily devotions. I even look forward to doing my chores. I am finding that I am completely enjoying my quiet time reading God's Word. For the first time in my life, I feel like God is actually talking to ME! I always "knew" of God, Jesus and all the stories but I never really "KNEW" God and I have such a hunger for Him now. I thank God everyday that I am His work in progress and I pray he never stops working in me until its time to go home and live with God.

God bless you and the outreach you have to spread the Word of God.

Dear

    I was 42 when I went thru the men's HOG. I, too, thought that I was such a low down, drug dealing, drunk, mean, jail bird, pervert, did not give a 'you know what' about nothing or nobody, that GOD could not and would not forgive me. I was WRONG. He forgave me, just like He did King David, murderer, liar, adulterer, Peter, big mouth, big head, denies JESUS 3 times and then there was Mary Magdalene, caught in the act of adultery, also had 7 demons. And last but not least, Paul, killer of Christians. God loves you ████████.

Give the Holy Spirit TIME to grow inside you. I've been in this walk for 8 years this April. It's still tough but, I Jn. 4:4. Also, I like this life MUCH better. Write me anytime. Love in Christ, Robert A. Smith

---

THE DEVOTION OF HEARING

"Samuel answered, 'Speak, for Your servant hears'" (1 Samuel 3:10).

Just because I have listened carefully and intently to one thing from God does not mean that I will listen to everything He says. I show God my lack of love and respect for Him by the insensitivity of my heart and mind toward what He says. If I love my friend, I will instinctively understand what he wants. And Jesus said, "You are My friends . . ." (John 15:14). Have I disobeyed some command of my Lord's this week? If I had realized that it was a command of Jesus, I would not have deliberately disobeyed it. But most of us show incredible disrespect to God because we don't even hear Him. He might as well never have spoken to us.

The goal of my spiritual life is such close identification with Jesus Christ that I will always hear God and know that God always hears me (see John 11:41). If I am united with Jesus Christ, I hear God all the time through the devotion of hearing. A flower, a tree, or a servant of God may convey God's message to me. What hinders me from hearing is my attention to other things. It is not that I don't want to hear God, but I am not devoted in the right areas of my life. I am devoted to things and even to service and my own convictions. God may say whatever He wants, but I just don't hear Him. The attitude of a child of God should always be, "Speak, for Your servant hears." If I have not developed and nurtured this devotion of hearing, I can only hear God's voice at certain times. At other times I become deaf to Him because my attention is to other things—things which I think I must do. This is not living the life of a child of God. Have you heard God's voice today?

FEBRUARY 13

← Takes time, be patient.

← Is. 30:21

← takes practice

Ps. 46:10

Pro. 30:5, Ps. 119:14

Good stuff
THE WORD of GOD, read it.
Ps. 16:11, 119:24, 32, 41-43, 50, 67, 71, 89, 97-105, 116, 148, 161, 16 165, 176. ☺ Have Fun. Ha!

Salvation

My Name is ██████████ I am a New Found Child of God. However, this wasn't always the case. I was born to a mother who was misguided and used cocaine. I was put into a foster home at age 2 and eventually adopted at age 5.

My new mom was addicted to marijuana. When she ran out of drugs, she became violent towards me. I began smoking marijuana at age 15. Later that year my mother beat me in a parking lot of a doctors office and I wound up in a girls home and later another foster home.

I found Jesus at the girls home and led the teenage music ministry my junior and senior year of high school. I moved away from god after I graduated when I met my first husband and got pregnant with my first son, ████.

My first husband was addicted to meth and I left him. (Not thinking marijuana was a problem). I met another man and had a child with him out of wedlock. I then got addicted to crack cocaine.

I moved from Texas to Mississippi after losing my children for drugs. I met my husband (now) and was "just smoking marijuana." His brother came home after my youngest son was born ██████. We were introduced to Meth at this time and our worlds spun out of control.

Wierd as it sounds, I always felt God

trying to pull me Home. One day I looked at
my husband and said, "I have to get the demons
out of me and I can't do it alone. We need
God in our lives to get us help."

Two days later, we were arrested and given
an opportunity to come to the Home of Grace.
God works in mysterious ways. I have been
here almost one month and my husband
refuses to allow his mom to post bond
until he has a bed available at the Home of Grace
men's home within 72 hours. God is Awesome!
He heard me even when I didn't think he
was listening.

Sincerely,

_____

RH's Note:
God is there, waiting,
watching and wanting
to help, if you will just
let Him. He can help
you get through
whatever is tearing
you apart.

Satan Went To Work On Me

Dear:

Sir's I would like to share with you how Jesus is working in my life. I was raised in a very good Christian home. As a boy our family regularly attended Baptist church. Both of my parent's loved Jesus and each other very much. They practiced their faith at home as well as in the various church homes they were called to serve in.

At the age of twelve I answered an alter call and gave my life to Jesus Christ, being a child in Christ at this age didn't bring about a lot of change. Being raised in a good home I was a relatively good child and didn't require a whole lot of attention. Not knowing much about repentance or what it meant, I did what most kid's that age would do. Nothing terrible but sin never the less. By the age of sixteen Satan really went to work on me, tempting me with girls, cigarette's, alcohol, drugs and money and I went for all of it. Believing the devil's lies I left home at sixteen quit high school in my senior year and began to do anything my flesh wanted me to do. With one semester to go and four school credits needed Satan would rob me of my high school graduation. After ten years of drug abuse and bad relationship's it was winter

I had gotten my G.E.D. but I had lost everything other than the clothes on my back, literally. Ten years of my life and everything I had ever worked for I had squandered. I turned to God, I was in trouble. Satan had robbed me of something more precious to me than gold while I wasn't looking. The date I had been saved.

Gathering all of the junk I had in my house I made a pile and burned it on the railroad tracks. Walking the isle at my parent's church ▮▮▮▮▮▮▮▮▮ Baptist church in O.K.C.) I would confess my sins and follow in believer's baptism. I was twenty six, ▮▮▮▮▮▮▮▮▮▮ I moved from the town I grew up in leaving my friends behind, I joined a local church (Williams Blvd. Baptist church in ▮▮▮▮▮▮▮▮) and got to work. I served faithfully for a while and God delivered me from the desire to use drugs. Something was missing from my life however, I was still smoking cigarettes you see, and I still hadn't fully repented to God, my walk with him stopped right there at the pack of smokes in my front pocket. Because of the stronghold Satan had on me through tobacco he had gotten back in my life and I didn't even know he was there. Life was good and before long I would be attending church less and less. I began to hang out with girls I shouldn't have and before long I would marry a non Christian girl. Soon a baby boy would come into our lives, years would pass as I went to school, concentrated on a career and making a good home for our child. I new I wasn't serving God and this deeply bothered me but life was good and I hadn't used drugs in over a decade now. I avoided my home church even more now because many times when I had gone the Holy Spirit would convict me to rededicate my life to Christ. I had ignored that calling for so many years" because of fear," that the spirit of God began to leave me alone. Satan had me right where he wanted me.

It was now ████ and life was catching up fast, after years of misery for not repenting and not giving up smoking I was knocking at the door of my old self. I spent most of ████ watching my ████████ father die of cancer and a hurricane destroy the gulf coast. I woke up one morning after a particularly rough night and looked in the mirror to find the old man was back and once again Satan had stolen the date on which I had walked the isle at ████████ Baptist church. Losing job after job I somehow made it back into the church and the Holy Spirit would begin to work on me again. Being led by God to a Billy Graham crusade I rededicated my life to Jesus. My family brought me to a secular detox program where I spent a few weeks then I returned home and tried to serve in a new church with a recovery program. I was still smoking and soon I would have a short series of relapses. This would some how land me at a Christian recovery camp called

As soon as my feet hit the ground the Holy Spirit began to convict me of my smoking. God spoke to my heart and demanded my obedience on this matter saying my walk with him could go no further, the fear of the lord was in my heart.

After lots of prayer and several attempts I was finally able to quit smoking with the help of Jesus. I have been tobacco free for five weeks and the joy of it is every day I have craving's that I can not overcome on my own. For twenty five years I smoked never missing a day I am completely convinced that I can not resist these terrible cravings without my savior Jesus Christ. God is working on many other areas of my life now because of my obedience in this one of smoking.

Almost every night in church he peels layers of my hardened heart and everyday he teaches me and reveals other areas of sin in my life.

God in his infinite wisdom knew that I would never be able to resist the temptation of drugs if I could not resist the temptation of smoking. I might resist for 15 years again if I lived but eventually I would go back.

If you hide your sins, you will not succeed but if you confess and reject them, you will receive mercy. Proverbs 28:13. ▮▮▮▮▮▮▮▮▮▮

▮▮▮▮▮▮▮▮▮▮▮▮▮▮▮▮▮▮▮▮▮▮▮▮▮ tell anyone who will listen, the truth I have just told you. My name is ▮▮▮▮▮▮ and

▮▮▮▮▮▮▮▮▮▮▮▮▮▮▮▮▮▮▮▮▮▮▮▮▮▮▮▮▮▮▮

Sexually Active at 14

Thank you for the books
and for taking time to show
your concern and that you care.
I would love a cool t-shirt
so hook me up with the best
one ya got! :) And a Bible
would be nice too. Some ladies
here have gotten one & I love
them - they're really nice Bibles!

Well, you said a 1 page
testimony so I'll skip details
and get straight to the point.
Otherwise, I'd be writing you
a book! I grew up & still presently
reside in ████████, MS. I grew
up with an amazing Christian
mother but an abusive father.
I firmly believed in God & I
know God is the only reason
my mother & I lived through
many traumatic nights. My
parents divorced when I was
12. Because of the divorce my
mom was looked down upon
by her church family. This
turned both of us away

from church. She became a
bad alcoholic ~~●●●●~~ and remarried
almost immediately. I turned
away from God COMPLETELY! I
started smoking weed & drinking
at age 12. By age 14 I was
sexually active, had rebelled
against family + ALL authority,
moved out & lived with friends &
did exactly what I wanted to do!
By 15 I had been introduced
to cocaine, meth, ecstasy, + pills.
~~●●●●~~ I lived with my boyfriend &
drug dealer & started saling drugs
to live. By 18 - I had started dating
another drug dealer living place to
place, had experienced the death of
a best friend to drugs & was in
a car wreck that killed an elderly
woman. However, I managed to
graduate high school! My step
dad had also died my senior
year, but I wasn't close to my
family enough to care at the time.
I had also went to jail for the
1st time at 17 for fighting at

school! Now - here I am - 19 years old & simple assault charges, 1 parafanelia charge, 1 manufactoring charge, 1 sales charge, 1 possession of illegal firearms charge, 1 shoplifting charge, and by the grace of God - I'm sitting in rehab praising God for his mercy & forgiveness to give me a 2nd chance at life & not 12 yrs. mandatory & 30 yrs' max in jail! After being in jail & here in rehab for the past 3 months I am sober - I have restored my relationship with God - I have broken all the strongholds holding me back from moving forward in life - and God has given me peace & happiness that I haven't known since I was a kid! God gave me the amazing talent to dance & I have begun to use this to worship Him! I plan to go back to school & pursue my dream of dancing & living for God!

However, school may have to be post-poned until the years of house arrest are concluded but I ~~know~~ know God will take care of me & put me exactly where it is that He wants me to be! I know God has plans for me because in all the small details that are left out - just know I should be <u>dead!</u> He has preserved my life for a reason! I have endured so much for a reason! I have faith that God allowed me to turn away & do things my way for a little while to show me that <u>my way was the wrong way</u>! I hit rock bottom & the only place to look was back up- to God! I hope to one day be able to share my testimony with people ~~⬤⬤~~ & change lives. Like I said before- this is the really short ~~⬤⬤~~ version. I know you probably have tons to read everyday! My graduation date is January ████ ████. I'm ready! God has very much so prepared me to go back out into the world & to be successful. Failure is no longer an option for me! God _is_ on my side! Thank you for your time! Let Mr. Headrick know I _greatly_ appreciate his time _as_ well. It is an honor for him to take time to ask you to send me books for my help! Thank you again!

God Bless,

Failure is **NOT**!!! an option!!!

She Shot At Me Four Times

I was brought up by the two best parents in the world and it all started in 80's when I was married to my first wife and we was not getting along and I started drinking alot and staying gone from home then I met my second wife she was a gal from meridian and her parents and grandparents owned the shop up their she was going to college to be a Reg. Nurse and she became a R.N. And she had two small babies and I had a little boy from first marriage. So she thought it would be good for me to be a Mr. Mom + it was great for a while then my brother introduced me to meth. thats when my life started going down hill. I started snorting meth on a regular basis and my wife was too, that went on for awhile then I could not get any for awhile cause the guy we was getting it from got busted and sent to prison so then my marriage was getting bad and then we had our daughter to get killed with the first car we bought her at sixteen! That sent us in

In a downward spiral. We split up &
Was still staying intouch. Then my brother
moved out to   in Ca. then we
Started dealing Meth from thier About 5oz.
A week And this went on for five or six years
And the law stopped my wife that was not living
with me and got her to try to set me up
She come And got me one Night And had
recorders under the seat Of her Car And
was Asking me to Let her get Something
And I Knew she was Acting funny so I told
her to Carry me to get Something to Eat
At burger King And she Kept Asking me to
get her something & Kept Saying what a talking
About so when we got to burger King she went
Crazy she told the girl at the drive through
that I was trying to Kill her so I got out
the Car And started walking when I got
to the back of her Car A gun went off.
She had shot At me with A 357 And missed
me thank God that was At 8 Feet At the
most of Coarse I ran Around the building
but then I had gotten really mad when I seen
I was not hit And she loved this New
Camaro ss So got her to Come Around

the building And She Shot At me
three more times. When I got her to
come on Around the building I ran
And Jumped In her Car And smoking
the tires was on I cut out. Anyway
I got down the road And stopped
The law come up And she Already had
Meth In her car to Set me up with
but It got thrown out At court Cause
A law man She was having Sex with give
her the gun And I tried getting back
On my feet And Nothing never worked
out to good then I met this young girl
Got her pregnant And had my baby girl
And started doing better in my
Life then kept falling back And she is five
Now And Its time to get my life right
And Im At the mission with the lord Jesus
Christ In My heart And washed me of All my
Sins. And getting Baptise
the of Aug. Cause he Is my Lord And I
hope he has A place for me In his world
                    love in lord
                    my Jesus

So Sad

my name is ███████ ███████ and I was
born in Buffalo New York on July ██████ I
spent the first 14 year in New York with both
of my parents who drank and fought very much
all of then time. My father served a year for DUI
and during that time his father was sick and I
came to Mississippi with him. My parents came here
about ██ year later. I quit school at the age of
16 to work and help my grandfather until he
passed. My parents still drank and fought. I got
my first wife pregnant at the age of 19 and got
married. I turned to drugs and alcohol then. I got
help at the age of 21 after getting a divorce from
her and met my second wife. I have a 14 year
old son with her but turned back to all the
drugs and alcohol. We also got a divorce after
a couple of years due to the alcohol but I had
pretty much left drugs alone due to going in and
out of jail. I have 1 child in between her and
my third wife by a woman I barely knew.
I see all my kids except him when I would.
~~I was~~ Me and my third wife had a good
relationship for about 3 years. I had my own
business and had Jesus in my life some and
he blessed me with 2 kids with her. When
I had Jesus in my life and was clean

I adopted one more child of hers. God made me a good person but I turned it back over to me and the devil. I lost my own business, my wife, and did not care about my kids. I thought I hit rock bottom but god gave me a chance with my 4th wife wich he has blessed me within her now. Her and god are the only hope I had and turned to again. I had put ████ "wife 4" threw so much and stayed in and out of jail. I spent everydime on bear and whiskey. My kids from ages 4 to 16 now said they loved me but would not see me drink my life away and would not see or talk to me at all. My wife had left and I lost my business again. Now I was at Rock Bottom at the county Jail for two DUI's in 1 week. One day I looked up and it was my anniversary and I was alone in Jail. I know I cried for an har and then begged god to help me. He was the only one I could turn to. I had got such a strange feeling that day after talking to god. I kept praying and 2 days later my wife got me out. I went to my parents for 2 days and the came to the ████████. God brought me here and has made me realize how much life has to offer me. My children have wrote me and I had my first christmas in along time thanks to god. I seen my kids smile and my wife is going to church so when I leave here I will already have a safe enviroment. I thank god everyday for the changes he has made in me and my family and just keep praying he will give me the strenght to keep living for him. I know with him I can have a life back but without him I am dumed. Sorry so long of a letter but maybe one day I can write one of glory and tell about my good changes happening because god is changing me and my life everyday.

Thank You

Large shirt and
Bible please. Have you   "God Bless"
got someway to let me know if you have anykind of books and how much. I enjoy reading now and would like some literature.

Something the Size of a Pea Ruined My Life

3 and a half years ago I came to my wife and told her what I was doing. She went to live with her parents while I could try to get my act together. A few weeks past and I was told about a "place". I figured I could go there, get cleaned, get my wife back in our home, get healed of my addition and my family and life would go back to normal. I was at this place for a month and when my wife came to see me, I knew I had her back! I knew I was clean! I "thought" I was healed from pills. So I left a happy man, went back home to my family. We were happy but only for a little while. Temptation came and I gave in. Since we both had the same bank account, it was hard for me to explain money missing. So I played it smart. I'd never take alot out at one time. Honestly, I wouldn't take pills every day or alot while I was married. She kept my problem at bay. I did this for well over a year before I got caught.

For the past few years, I've lived for satan. I let something the size of a pea control my thinking, my life, my decisions, everything about me was surrounded by pills. It was extremly bad when I'd have a bad day or going through something stressful. I'd always find what I thought was "peace" in a pill or even a few strong drinks. I was lying to my wife, my family and my friends. Looking back now; maybe I lied about my addiction to pills or made excuses because I knew deep down inside the life and person I was, was not me. I was hoping that I would wake up one day and be healed and everything would go back to normal. I was wrong. The more I tried to fight the battle alone, the worst the battle got. The more I kept it inside, the bigger the problem got. I was very smart with hiding my addiction from everyone. But little by little my world fell apart. Soon good friends left me, then family relationships began to crack.

When she found out again, she asked
me for a divorce. Only when I found
out she was seeing someone else, my addiction
went from bad to the worst of worst. I
wanted to die. I really don't know how
I made it alive this past year. Satan
had a plan for me, but Jesus had another
plan. Since coming to "Mission at the cross",
I've found peace through returning to Jesus
and letting him use me and seeking his
will for my life. I couldn't be more
happier even when I've lost everything
I worked hard for. I'm letting Jesus
build my life back the way he wants
it. God is in control of my life. I still
at times have bad days, but I don't run
to a pill for peace, I go to the cross.

The Battle Still Rages

Hi. My name is ▆▆▆▆▆▆▆. I was born in Chattanooga, TN ▆▆▆▆▆▆, ▆▆. I am 25 years of age. I had a great childhood and great adolecent years as well. My parents are wonderful people and my sister is as well. I grew up in a middle class neighborhood. My parents did pretty good financially. I'd say around the age of 14 or 15 I took my first drink. Up until I was about 17, I never really drank but 2 or 3 times after that. When I was 18, I took my first drug. I was dating a girl I went to high school with. I forgot to add that I moved from Tennessee to Mobile Al when I was about ten. Sorry. Anyway, we were dating for a few months and man did I think I was in love. Well, she dumped me. I was hurting. She broke my young, enexperienced heart. My buddy and I hung out that weekend. His name is ▆▆▆▆. He offered me this pill that he called ecstacy. He said it would make me feel better. It did. After that it was all down hill. From the ages of 18-22, I was addicted to ecstacy, cocain, and crystal meth. My meth addiction was by far the worst. I of course drank like a fish all those years along with the drugs. Fortunately, I kicked the drug habit on my own →

before I had a chance to know Christ, so
I gave myself all the credit and little did
I know, it was Him who delivered me
from it. I still drank just about
every day though up until I started
my stay(s) here at this Recovery Center
Back to ████, my buddy that I was
involved in drugs with, he passed away
December ████████. He walked out of
a bar and was struck by a vehicle. I was
devastated. This was my best friend since
I was 15 years old. After his death I was
just a mess for months and months. I drank
and drank, and drank. I finally accepted
the fact he's not comin back, but that
I would see him again one day. Through
the years of the drugs and alchohol, I
never really cared too much about anything
but myself. I was a selfish, prideful,
sad excuse for a human being. ████
████████████████████████████████████

It even got so bad the past two years
that I attempted suicide 3 times by
overdose on different medications I would
steal out of my parents medicine cabinet.
I came extremely close 1 particular time.
That was when I said I've had enough.
I want to be happy. I want to get
married one day and start a family
of my own and live a life full of joy.
Jesus Christ told me I could. Thats why
I'm dedicating the rest of my life to Him. →

Life is wonderful and I'm thankful for God's grace and mercy He has humbly bestowed upon me. I thank you for your time, and who knows? Maybe this testimony can be an inspiration to someone. But I do know that the struggle isn't over. I know I will battle things the rest of my life but with Jesus Christ in my life I will always know victory will be waiting for me!

RH's Note: God gives us the privilege to make our own choices, but He does not give us the privilege to determine the consequences of our choices.

The Solution is Jesus

Dear Mr. Smith,

Hello, My name is ▓▓▓▓▓▓▓. I'm nineteen years old and a client of the ▓▓▓▓▓▓▓. I heard about Hellfighters through one of the other clients and I was wondering if you would send me one of those cool t-shirts and Bible. I would also like to give you my testimony.

I was born December ▓▓▓▓▓ to your average middle-class unhappy family. After thirteen years of feeling sorry for myself I started doing drugs. I've used almost every drug out there and the quantity steadily increased over the years. When I turned seventeen all hell broke loose, and by the time I turned eighteen I started getting notorious with all the cops in my area. Now I have a rap sheet hanging over my head that no nineteen year old should have.

My mother has been praying for me for years now. I actually think my increased dissention made her faith stronger. I told her when I was eighteen that I was an atheist. I could literally feel her heart break. I'm not sure why I was trying to piss God off, but in the back of my mind ▓▓▓▓▓ I've always known He was real.

He started dealing with my heart in small ways around the beginning of '▓▓ Whether it was by sending one of His followers to talk to me, or putting certain "coincidences" in my lap. One day I broke down and started praying. I asked God to help me see what I was supposed to be doing.

I had no clue what I was asking! About a week later I was in jail facing prison. The judge wanted to teach me a lesson, but then something happened. My mother started doing her research and found a place called the ████████. Within a day I was accepted into the program. I've been told that I better not show my face back in a Justice Court unless I wanted 3-5!

I arrived at the ██████████ on the ██ of April. My first day here I wanted to fight ████████. So obviously I was still struggling with my authority problems, and I'm sure Joe ██████ can also testify to that! I'm not gonna lie, I was angry. I'm sure I made some good first impressions during weeks zero and one. During week two we had a revival. A H.O.G. Alumnist named Dewayne was the speaker. I'm still not sure if it was divine intervention or what but for some reason what he was saying made sense. I would go to my room after chapel to read my Bible and I finally understood what it was saying. Some time during that week I had a long talk with God. I've never found a drug that could give me the peace I now have.

I still have problems with anger and authority but with the help of God and my brothers in Christ I can overcome any obstacle. As far as lif after Christ goes, I don't know what God has in store for me, but I hope it's something great.

A Sinner Saved by Grace

P.S. - I graduate July 20th and I wear a size Large t-shirt.

THE WAY OF LIFE
Obedience

As Dr. Parker says, "A child can treat God with sulkiness and silence. The tiniest knee can stiffen and refuse to bow before Him."

"Strive to enter in at the strait gate." "I will not."

"Look unto me and be ye saved." "I will not."

"Come unto me, and I will give you rest." "I will not."

"Seek ye first the kingdom of God." "I will not."

"Repent." "I will not."

"Turn ye, turn ye, why will ye die?" "I will not."

"Believe in the Lord Jesus Christ." "I will not."

"Give me thine heart." "I will not."

"Go work in my vineyard." "I will not."

"Remember the Sabbath day to keep it holy." "I will not."

"Lay up for yourself treasures in heaven." "I will not."

So we might go through the Bible, and we would find that rebellious man refuses to obey His commandments and follows the devices and desires of his own heart. God made man for His glory, but man joined the devil and became a rebel.

Now this is the question to be settled. The battle is fought on that one word of the will; the door hangs on that one hinge of the will. Will you obey? That is the question! Will you obey the voice of God and do as He commands you? No man can obey for you any more than he can eat and drink for you. You must eat and drink for yourself, and you must obey God for yourself.

God requires literal, prompt, cheerful obedience. Nothing less will do. If you changed the doctor's prescription only a little, you might turn it into rank poison. A Sunday school teacher once asked her class, "How is the will of God done in heaven?"

One child answered, "Cheerfully."

Another, "By everybody."

A third, "All the time."

But the best answer was, "It is done without asking any questions."

D. L. MOODY

Dear

Rebel. Man, so much of your story reminds me of me. Mainly, I took no B.S. off of anyone. When I was your age, the first time I got pulled over while drunk & stoned, I punched & kicked the Chief of Police of a town just south of Dallas, Tx.

Needless to say, after being handcuffed and put in the back seat, I was given a 'lesson' on why you don't assault the police, Ha. A very painful lesson. ⬛, I say that not to brag, but to teach. My 'lil' brother, I was BLESSED to live long enough to make it to the H.O.G. in '98. I was walking death when I got there. I've done all the hard stuff, herion, LSD, Quays, Preys, Crank, Crank, Crystal, Wiskey, Vodka, ect... I've drank drugs, smoked em, shot em up my arm, snorted em up my nose, inhaled em, played with demons by talking with em, been in jail

(over)

no less than 20 times, been in I don't know how many wrecks, had guns pulled on me, fights, friends die from O.D., wrecks, drug deals. Man, I've done dope, grown dope, sold dope, WHICH ALL THIS I SAID, MAKES ME A DOPE!! Satan's dope. Man, it's all a lie. That, my 42 years was not fun, not exciting, not life, it was all the road to death, misery, pain, loneliness, HELL. ████, IT'S ALL A LIE. Man, you are only 19. STOP running from God. Oh, if only in 1974 I could have found the Home of Grace. But, ████, it's not the H.O.G., it's JESUS. As a tree needs sun and water to live, so we need JESUS. Man, I don't think I've ever sent anyone all the pictures & stuff I sent you. The Holy Spirit, I think, is telling you thru me, "STOP, ████, listen to me." ████, I still deal with alot but I have Jesus on my side. Road rage, anger, temptations, desires. Pro. 25:28. Memorize it. I Pt. 2:21. Live it. It's your choice. Be like Joshua, "...as for me and my house, we will serve the LORD." Josh. 24:15 Write me anytime. My cell # is on the back of my tract, Son of a Preacher Man. Love In Christ, Robert A. Smith
Matt. 6:21
Ps. 147:3

Then My Parents Divorced

This is My TesTimoney

First let me say it's been a long journey. It all started in 9th grade skinny litter boy trying to be cool like everyone else. So i went and smoke my first joint. Boy i though i was the cooless guy at school, but i was still going to class. Then 10th grade came my parent got a divorce. we was a happy family other kids was jerlous we went on trips together the movie together the best clothes everything and then it was over. So then i went to hanging out with gangs and drinking and smoking reed next thing i Know i was hook. Then 11th grade came and i though i was bad so i drop out of school, but i got a job. Then i went to tooting cocaine and it was fun at the time i ...ad money, girl and drugs i though i was on top of the world. But when the money ran out i started taking people money to get high. I hurt a lot of people i'm 42 years old now and still cun't sleep at night for the things i don't all for drugs. It wasn't me i was brought up in a good church my father was a preacher i sing in the choir; song in church concerts, but when you let drugs come in thats a whole different thing. I ended up in jail, then i found Jesus again and he made me a promise i would

change my life around, but then i let the
demon come back in this time i was married and
had four kid who love me to death, but i still kept
on drinking and doing cocaine, stealing, I lost alot
of good jobs and good cars. My life was a mess.
So i went and got help for 30 days. I did good
there was know more cocaine in my life but i was
still drinking not that much that was back in
1996. Then bang my mother and my wife past
away 2 month apart mother in october and wife
in december. I wanted to kill myself so many
time. I started drinking twice as much nonstop,
I lost another job, but i ~~don't~~ didn't go back to
cocaine just drinking trying to drink myself to
death i heard of the rehab center and for 3 month
it kept on coming to my head off and on, but i was
just to depress them ~~leaving~~ me hurt so bad. So one
night at 12:30 at night i pull out my gun put i to
my head and then ... my friend son came in
the door and ran straight to me now that was scary.
How did he know to come buy so take my gun home
with him. and then the recue centers name kept
coming up in my head, There is got to be something
to all this so here i am. And i'm starting to feel

better about myself allready. I'm trying to fine the lord all over again and this time find my purpose he has for me thank you for listening to me. There is alot more to this story but i don't want to take up all your time God Bless you.

your Truly

There's Nothing God Can't Do!

████████, Hellow my name is █████████ ████████. I'm from ████████ MS, NeXT TO M°ComB. I am 31 years old. I am curenTly aT a Christian RehaB. I am wriTing TO give you my STORY. my RoommaTe TolD me abouT you, I was iNTResTeD anD LiKeD The ██████████ you senT him. I TO would LiKe Sum iNFORMaTion on waT Ya'll Do, and waT Ya'll STanD FOR. I wanT TO Join a ChRisTian CLUB anD Share my STORY wiTh oTheRS, and LeT PeoPLe Know how PowerFULL goD ReaLy iS!! my STORY STaRTS wenTI was a young Teen. I cum From a SoLiD Christian FamiLy. BuT you couLDNT Tell By waT I was Doing. aT home, church, or arrouND PeoPLe ThaT Knew my PareNTS I was a SaiNT! I DiD No wrong. (ha, ha, ha.) I TolD my seLF, I goT ya'll FooLeD! BuT waT I FaiLD To ThinK abouT was GOD! I Saw iT years LaTTeR. OK. I STaRTeD LiKe eveRY oTheR Teen. EXSPeremeNTiNG, wiTh SeX, Drugs, anD Beer. YuP I was The CooL KiD! wen I goT my FIRST CaR, O ya iT was ReaLy on Then. I haD money, So I haD aLL The BesT FRieNDS. aLL The BesT DrugS, aLchahoL, PReTTiesT giRLS, I haD iT aLL! (So I ThaughT) ha. one niTe my PareNTS weT on a ████ LayReNewel weekenD, ouT of Town.

So I did like all "good Teenage boys,"
I had a party! all my "best" friends
came. That nite I met my wife. we dated
a few years, got married, had 2 boys. I had
a great 2 faced life. I learned latter
after 5 years of marriedge, that she did to.
Ya I was at church one nite doin the
"good boy thing" but it was different this
time. god spoke to my heart. I was saved!
So I went home and told my wife. She
told me she wasen't cuming to watch me
get baptised! god couldn't love me! I didn't
desirve it cus. of the way I was living.
I tryed fer 3 days to show and tell her
that god could love and save me. It didn't
work! So I got baptised by myself, she was
at home "I thaught". you see I worked on
a Towe Boat on the miss. River, I was gone
30 days home 30 days. made good money, but
wen I came home, I had no money. so
I got nosey about things. I learned that
wile I was cleaning up my life, that
she was loosing hers. She got hooked on
meth! It destroyed our marriage. I
took it all out on god! Thats wen I
went off the Deep end.

I DID THE OPOSIT OF JOB. I COURSED
GOD AND WANTED TO DIE! I CAME REAL
CLOSE A FEW TIMES, BUT I THAUGHT OF MY
2 BOYS. I SAYD IF THERE MOM DIES AND I
DIE WHO'S GUNA TAKE CARE OF THEM? THATS
WEN I BACKED DOWN. I KNOW NOW IT WAS
THE HOLY SPIRIT PUTIN THOSE THAUGHTS IN MY
HEAD. I WAS TO HIGH TO THINK THAT MYSELF.
WE HAD A 3 YEAR BATTLE IN COURT OVER OUR
KIDS. EVEN THOUGH I WAS LIVING OF THE
WORLD, AND LIKE JOHNA RAN FOM GOD AS
FAST AND HARD AS I COULD, HE WAITED. I
KEPON WINNING THE COURT CASES EVERY TIME,
I EVEN GOT PAYED BACK THE "CHIALD SUPORT
THAT I PAYED HER. GOD IS GOOD THEN ONE DAY
I GOT THAT PHONE CALL! YUP YOU GOT IT.
SHE WAS KILLED IN A CAR WRECK. SO I HAD TO
TELL THE BOYS THAT MAMA WASENT GUNA
CUM GET THEM NO MORE. IT TORE ME UP!
AND IT PUTE ME EVEN DEEPER. BUT GOD
WAITED." SO THEN I WENT TO NEW STRONGER
DRUGS. I WANTED ANSWERS, AND COMFORT.
THEN ONE DAY I CAME HOME FROM THE
RIVER PARTYING ALL DAY!! MY DAD BRAUGHT
MY KIDS TO ME, THEY HAD SCHOOL THE NEXT
DAY.

I made supper, they ate and got ready fer bed. My youngest boy huged an kissed me good nite. Then he told me "Dady I love you, but I dont love you wen you drink all the beers in the blue and white cans." That broke my heart. So I tried. A.A. no good. I tried. N.A. again no good. I tried by myself (ha wat a joke that was). Then a friend asked me to go to church with them, I sayed ok. God started to move on me that day. So I ran again. I went out partied harder than I have ever before. I was ready to end it all. But god sayed no! not yet. I had a bad wreck and could have died. I took out a lite pole, and a coulvert in my jeep. No seat belt or nuthing. My head went through the windshield, my chest hit so hard on the steering wheel that I broke the steering collum in half, and bent the wheel in the shape of a taco. Wen the cops got there I blew in the toob. I blew a 3.75 I was border line dead from poisoning. But by gods grace I only got 9 stitches in my head.

No Broosing or Pain. I went To
CourT and BeeT The D.U.I. Chg That
I had. I was Free again. I STayed That
way FeR 2 years afTer That Day. Then
one Day my DaD TOLD me aBouT a Christian
Recovery centerI Laughed aT him, TOLD him
I DiDnT have a ProBlem. 3 Days LaTTer
I went ouT and saw an X girL friend of
mine, and goT in a Rage, and went home.
I wrecked my Truck again un hurT. I
called my DaD To cum geT me, and wen
he DiD I Lashed ouT aT him. he Drove
me home and I PreVoKeD him unTill
we haD a FisT FiTe. again I was in
Jail. I BroKe Down, (or shoulD I say goD
BroKe me Down) wen I goT ouT I TOLD
him I wanTeD To go To The rehaB.
he sayeD OK, I'll geT you There. BuT
since Then Because we serve a
goD OF seconD Chances, and a verry
PaTianT goD. I have since ran BacK
To goD! he has BLesseD me so much!
he weLcomeD me with oPen armes!
I am geTing soBeR, I FixeD my RelaTionshiP
with my DaD, and FamiLy. goD has BLesseD
me with new FrienDS, a new LiFe,
and a new Beginning.

With This New Beginning I am
working For The Lord, and I want
People To Know That we are Different
in every way That god Loves Them
For Them, Not For wat They have or
havent Dun. Theres Nothing god Cant
Do! in Colossians 1:21-22 says and
you That were some Time alienated and
enemies in your minde By wicked works
Yet Now hath he reconciled, in The
Body of his Flesh Through Death To
Present you holy and unBlamable and
unreprovable in his sight. I have
Forgiveness For my Life B Jesus Blood.
I am Thankefull Fer That. and Thats
my Story in a nut shell. So Let me Know
how or wat I can Do To help Yalls
ministery.

Thank you.
May god Bless!

They Let ME Teach Your Kids

Today, Jan. 27, ▓▓, I can say that I am "born again". I can say I've had 31 days clean and sober! However, the road to salvation has been long and dark!

I was raised in a Presbyterian church. I proclaimed my faith in God at the age of 12. ("Everyone did it"!) But I was never really "Born again" until I found Jesus right here! I first played around with drinking and "pills" as a teen. I didn't drink "EVERY DAY" so I "didn't have a problem". I held down a 10 year career at ▓▓▓▓▓▓ Bank working from Teller, New accts, CD's IRA's to being a Loan Closer. Looking back, I had big issues! I missed work often due to hangovers! (I still didn't have a problem, cuz I didn't do it "EVERY DAY").

I ~~went to~~ left ▓▓▓▓▓▓ Bank and went to USA Insurance Co. because I'd make more money going in the door. By this time I had been married, divorced and remarried - to the same wonderful man - within a year! We were very on and off. If we disagreed (and most married people do), I

just left. If I didn't get my way
I was gone. I was lost and searching
for "something" but I didn't know what.
We'd go to church on and off. I "knew"
God. But I wasn't living like it. I went
to God in times of need!

Things began getting really bad when
I stumbled on to the "high" of mixing pain
pills and alcohol. The more depressed I
was the more unstable I became. I left
▓▓▓▓ To go to work for my sons school.
▓▓▓ He was going to kindergarten and I wanted
school hours and holidays so this was
really convenient. (No one knew I was about
to get fired ▓▓▓▓▓▓ due to my "medication
and alcohol binges)

I was at the school as an assistant
teacher for almost five years. But
the last 2 of the five were horrible..
My husband got fed up with the drinking
and medication so he divorced me for the
third time. I got arrested for public
drunk. I was forced to resign from the
school because of that incident + My son's
last day of school before Christmas holidays
I was supposed to pick him up, well I did
something, as a mother, I've never done.
I fell asleep and didn't hear the phone!
They had to bring him to me. That was it.
They called my ex husband and told him
I could no longer pick up my son. He also
found out I'd been hiding the fact that I
didn't have a job. They found a good →

recovery program and said they wouldn't involve DHS if I went for help.

I was really angry at first. But the best Christmas present I ever got was knowing that I was going to a safe place. Knowing that I was saved by the grace of Jesus Christ our Lord.

I was at the recovery center a week. I was happy. I was doing the right thing. I was forgiving myself and really making progress. But something kept bothering me. I didn't really know that I know that I know, I was going to Heaven! I had fears and I was resisting "something". Well, we had devotion one night - It was as if God was speaking directly to me! I hadn't truely surrendered! I went to the alter call. I am the most free, peaceful, sure person that I know! I know, that I know that I KNOW - Jesus payed the price for my sins. I'm not looking back. I'm confessed. I'm repenting and I'm praising the most glorious, wonderful, precious, person that I know = God!

I don't know what his full plan is for me yet. I'm been here three weeks. After I'm gotten what I'm gotten in 3 weeks, I can't imagine what he has in store for me when I graduate! I know that I will be "giving back" what I'm been given. I do plan to speak and do some sort of counseling. It will be more clear as I meditate, pray and learn

$\rightarrow$

312

more of "His Word". I am praying for
restoration of my relationship with
my exhusband! He has turned to God.
He is a wonderful man and I hope
God allows me to give back to him
some of what I've been blessed to learn here!

Thank you and
God Bless –

Dear Robert,

Thank you so much for the bible and everything else that you sent to me.

I've recieved alot of things since I've been locked up. But for some reason that little bible moved and touched my heart.

I've been here at ███████ since Sept. ~~of this year~~ and have been locked up since aug. I'm scheduled to get out in Dec ██ I've been saved for a long time (since I was a child) but for many years I've been druging & drinking and every thing that goes with it.

In Sept. I decided I was screwing up my life and obviously so because I'm sitting in prison. ~~It~~ At first I still balked at going to Church because I didn't just want jail house religion But God literally kept pulling at me and finally I smartened up. Now I'm in a faith base dolm and I'm learning how to walk with the Lord again. Already he has put many blessings in my life! your bible was one of them. I really want to continue to grow in Christ but I have so many questions. Even though

I'm in a faith base dorm it' just diffrent from someone on the Outside maybe somebody more like me, I can't explain it. Sometimes I feel unworthy because I dont yell or jump around filled with the Holy Ghost. I know that I love and believe in Jesus Christ, I believe God has a plan for my life and I want to worship and walk with him.

I'm 48 year old addict (crack cocaine and a alcholic) I lived in Panama City FLA (Bay Co) I'm a commercial fisherman (woman) and am very good at what I do. I dont know if I will continue to fish or not.

My fiance' is very supportive and is also a Christian He is a blessing in my life. In so many ways I am very fortunate. But I am so thirsty for a spiritual leader or sombone that I can communicate with that I "click" with. I'm not saying the girls here are'nt good and most are christian like but sometimes I feel like they dont understand me.

I would love to hear from you or anyone you feel would be good for me to communicate with. There is so much I want to learn, I have no church and some times I just feel like I'm drifting along.

Please write Back
I would to & like to hear more from you.

I'll be waiting to hear from you.

Vodka Was My Demon's Name

I was born in the late 1950's in small town Mississippi. We were one of those families who were poor, as most were in those days, but never knew it because of the love. Church was never missed whether it be Sundays, Wednesday revivals, socials, youth camps, etc...

When I was 12, our preacher walked into our vacation bible school class and asked how many of us boys wanted to go to heaven. All ten of us raised our hands, and we repeated the salvation prayer with him. While our pastor probably mistakenly added to his count of souls won for Christ, which many do, he did do right by getting the ball rolling. We raced down to the front of the church the next Sunday, joined it and were baptized. The kid who kept us in trouble most of the time even had a shirt on that said "The devil made me do it." I was no more saved then than he proved to be. However, after much conviction, the following Tuesday night I got on my knees and asked God to save me. I knew it immediately.

I was just a normal kid in every way. graduating highschool, jr college, and senior college while working 40 plus hours a week. I got married, had children, divorced and repeated it all again in the 90's. I made many mistakes and strayed often, but I never doubted my salvation or relationship with God.

In the late 90's, I decided my life needed a change of direction. I went with my children on a field trip to Washington, DC. When I woke the first morning, I knew something was wrong. I ate countless oranges and drank orange juice at the breakfast bar, vomited it up and kept repeating it. We went to the Capital, met with Trent Lott and I fell out. I tried to stand but my legs would not hold me up. If you ever want your picture taken, come out of the US capital building on a stretcher. I didn't make the newspaper though. After sitting for hours in the emergency room and having tests run, the doctor finally came in. I asked him what was wrong. He said it was simple; "I didn't have enough alcohol in me".

For while my story seemed pretty normal, what I didn't tell you was that I had never missed drinking two ½ gallons of vodka per week for the last fifteen years. In order to graduate college, you have to have speech. I had tried several times before but had always dropped it before the first speech. As a senior in college I would have gladly taken some advanced physics class instead. But; no speech grade, no diploma. I fixed a drink on the morning of my first speech and could have spoken on national TV. I passed with flying colors.

My tolerance for alcohol was very high, and the intoxicating habit made all of life easier. It just became a part of my everyday life. A spiked drink was always close by. I never got drunk but I guess was never completely sober. I never saw the wrong, even if it was before church or while reading my Bible.

The shock of no alcohol in Washington led to the DT's which I remember perfectly. I decided that night that I was walking home. A cop stopped me and informed me that my hospital gown had no back in it, and I certainly didn't have no underware on. He cuffed me and brought me back. I have no recollection after that, but they told me I tried to escape again before dawn. The strength of the human body in this condition is unreal. Security caught me and had been trying to strap me down on a leather table for fifteen minutes when my wife walked in. I snapped out of it immediately and was allowed to go back to my room. The three men said I had beat the stew out of them. I remember a nurse telling me I was in for a very hard time if I drank again.

Not enough alcohol in me? I tanked up on the trip home. I drank for nine months before it caught up with me again. Alcoholism is progressive. The next time it took only six, then three, then one,

and in the end, just one day before having to
be detoxed.

The next 4 or 5 years was a continuous process
in and out of treatment centers. I called an
ambulance to my house three times. I tried both
christian and secular treatment centers, switched
around to different churches, went to AA, and
prayed constantly to God for help. Still I never
managed more than a month or so sober. Depression and financial trouble are killers for an
addict, and every way I turned seemed hopeless. I repeatedly threw half empty bottles
out through the woods only to find myself
crawling around at 3AM looking for them.
I made the mistake once of pouring it all out.
at 4 AM I tried to disguise the beer with
milk, eggs, and bread. The cashier would
not sell it to me. I went to five stores
before finally grabbing a 12 pk. The clerk
told me they couldn't sell it before 6 AM
before I even got to the counter. I laid a
twenty on the counter and told her I was
an alcoholic but not a thief. I was gone
before the cops arrived.

It wrecked my car once and when I
ran out of vodka, I rode a bike ten
miles to town. I was shaking so
bad that I couldn't make it to the liquor
store. I stopped by a curb store and
had to let the cashier get my money
out of my wallet. I went around back
and got a truck driver to open one up

for me, and I managed to get half of it down and half on me. The shakes subsided long enough for me to get to the package store only to find out I had no way to carry it. I bought two pints, went around back and drank one, rode back home and drank the other one, and brought a backpack back and bought six 1/2 gallons.

During one stretch, I was having to fix a drink at lunch just to make it to the end of my work shift. My boss who knew all about me found out and told me I couldn't do that. I washed out a three ounce nose spray bottle and filled it with vodka. I would suck it down at lunch and it would give me just enough to make it til I got off.

One time I had been sober for a few weeks but lost it on a weekend. I called the guy I was working with and told him I would be late coming in Monday. I had messed up. When I awoke at 3:00 AM, I quickly called him to apologize for sleeping so late. He asked me if I knew what day it was. I said Monday. He said no it was Wednesday. A friend of mine said we had talked in the package store Monday night, and he tried to talk me out of buying it. He never knew I had been drinking.

I actually think I experienced the demons of Proverbs 23 once while detoxing. I had gone 24 hours with nothing to drink when

I cut the lights off to try to sleep. There were millions of flys all over the ceiling. I would cut the lights on and they would be gone. I was lying there looking at them when six demon like creatures came through the back door and wall. They looked like gremlins with four being male and two having female characteristics. The females were the worst. They flew and grabbed at my neck while the males just punched on me. They were as real as anything I have ever seen. I flipped the light switch constantly and finally just left it on. Even though I was alone, I was embarrassed that I was actually swinging at them. I thought I was crazy. The next night I cut the lights off and the flies were gone. A few minutes later, here they come through the back door. I cut the light on and got down on my knees and asked God to help me. Then I cut the light off and put my hands behind my back and said go for it. I am sure I looked like an idiot flailing around but after a little while, the leader just looked at me and said thats it. lets go and they left. I got up and drank some water and took a shower. Then I cut the lights out and went to sleep. I knew the DT's were over. A lot of people die of heart failure while going through this. Your blood pressure is off the charts. If I had of died, my autopsy would have showed absolutely no alcohol involved in it.

An addict can tell a hundred stories of the horrors, but none are important as how you quit. I deeply respect AA, but the idea that any god will do never let me reap its benefits. On the night of my last meeting, a man stood up and said that he didn't know if God was a he, a she, or an it, but God kept him sober for two years. I could barely make two weeks. My belief was always that the devil never messed with those who didn't know the true god. He already had their souls. Making a christian stumble is what he loves. I think he could care less about a devil worshiper with jet black spiked hair, black leather clothes, and 666 tattooed all over him. But let him make a TV evangelist or catholic priest or any other religious person fall. That is his best work.

The next day feeling lonely and depressed out of my mind, I started drinking. I woke up in the drunk tank with no idea how I got there or what I had done. For the first time since I was twelve, I doubted my salvation. An alcoholic has three choices. He can be sobered up, locked up, or covered up. There is no alternative. My father wanted to come get me, but I said no. I spent ten days in jail developing a plan. I got mad. I got angry. I got assurance from God that I was saved and began. It was all or nothing.

To some peoples surprise, it did not start with God but with me. I made up my mind

100%. No more games. No more asking God to help me quit while handing the liquor store owner a twenty. And not to my surprise, God started helping.

I printed a list of items to be read every-day. The first was ~~████~~ Philippians 3:13 where Paul was forgetting the past and moving on. Paul's past was much worse than mine. I wrote Matthew 6:25-27 where Jesus said don't worry about tomorrow. An addict carries tremendous guilt so I wrote several down where God forgives all 100%.

I made a list of things for me to do just to be a better person. One was to say a small prayer every time I hear a siren, see someone broke down, or walking down the highway. All of them usually need a prayer and it brings you back to God when He is the farthest thing from your mind. Always give a small donation to anyone who asks. If you have doubts about them, what they do with the money is between them and God. You are following God's command to help widows and orphans (needy). No littering on the highway, develop patience at Walmart. All of this has made me a better person. Always go to church and read the bible daily, even when you don't want to. I quit watching depressing news and television programs.

I did whatever it took to stay sober including staying at home if that was

what it needed to do, or leaving home if
that was what it needed.

And last of all 'The Snake'

A man was walking down a sidewalk on
a cold winter day when he saw a snake.
The snake asked him to pick him up and
put him in his coat so he could warm up.
The man told him he couldn't because he was
a snake and would bite him. The snake
promised him he wouldn't, so the man did
it. The snake bit him and he slung him
down saying you said you wouldn't bite me.
The snake said: "You Know What It Was
When You Picked Me Up."

My snake was staying at home and
getting depressed or leaving home going
where I shouldn't be going, plus a few
others. We all have snakes. A gambling
addict can't go to a casino 'just to eat.'
A drug addict can't hang around with his
old friends. If your butt is too big,
you can't admire the different new flavors
of Blue Bell at Walmart. The snake will
bite everytime. It was several years after
it sobered up that I even thought about
the devil being portrayed as a snake
in the Bible. No wonder it works.

Throughout the years of my sobriety now, I often look back at 15 years of a gallon of liquor a week and wonder why I am alive. My doctor said I shouldn't be but I am. I believe it is because God has a plan and a reason for everything. I am paying for my sins by struggling to be a single parent. This is not the way God intended for us to live, but where would my child be now if it was dead. God knew my son would need me when I thought all I needed was another drink. Only God knows what else I may be needed for one day, and because of them, I live!

Praise the Lord

What a Mess I Made

Dear Hellfighters,

My name is ████████████. I live in ████████████, La. I heard about your organization through people at the recovery facility where I currently am at. This is the first time I have given my testimony so, please bear with me.

I was born on October 9, ████ in ████████████ at ████████ Memorial Hospital. My childhood was a good one, some would say priviledged. I went to a catholic church growing up. My mother made me and my sisters go up until about middle school. That is where the drugs came in. It started out as a little bit of weed. When I got into high school the bottom fell out. I started doing perscription drugs extasy, and finally my worst downfall cocaine. I stayed on drugs during all of my high school years, hard. When I graduated in ████ I had all the grades to go to college but I didn't. I was too wrapped up in the low life of drugs and alcohol. I got a job straight out of high school as a carpenter helper for a framing crew. It was fast money, no drug test, it was what I looking for at the time. What I didn't know then it would also bring me no future. It paid good and all. but working for cash with no benefits, 401k, or retirement plans. is not the best career choice. I was not trying to hear it though, I just wanted to get high. With a crew full of convicts and dopeheads I was in the right place. So I thought then. I continued with this destruction and downward spiral, basically up until January ████, I'll get back to that.

During the summer of ████ I was at home alone and was eating Zanex. That and cocaine were my drugs of choice. I decided to break into a house and steal some guns. I did it. A couple weeks later the Police came to my house and arrested me. They found my fingerprints at the scene. I was booked into ████████ Parish Jail Complex for Poss. of a Stolen Firearm,

altering numbers on a firearm, and burglary.
If convicted on all, was facing about
20 years. My family came into play and
got me a good lawyer. By the grace
of God the gun charges were dropped,
but I was still up for the burglary.
My lawyer got me a plea bargin,
I would get 4 years home incarceration
for the burglary if I would plead
guilty. So I did it. I just wanted
to go home.

    Now I am a convicted felon on
4 years house arrest on the streets
with an ankle braclet on doing the
same things that burnt me in the
first place. I was not respecting the
house arrest at all, still doing drugs,
still in the spiral going down. In ~~January~~
June ~~███████~~ I violated my home
incarceration. I was granted a technical
violation and a 90 day turnaround in
Parish Prison. I was happy but still
blind. ~~███████~~, on my birthday, I
got out of jail. First thing I did
was go get high + drunk. Everyone, including
myself, knew it was only a matter of
time before I violated again and

went back to Jail. If revoked I would serve 4 years DOC* time in a La. Prison. I didn't care. I was dumb. Went back to the same job, same friends, same Disaster. So time came when the police came to my door again. I didn't say much, I went quietly. This was in January of ███. I thought I was done for this time. I was told I wouldn't be given another chance. I remained in Jail. Court date in Feb; nothing new, Court date in April, just another continuance. Finally in May I called my mother and she told me that they would allow me to go to a rehab center in Miss. called the Home of Miracles I thought great, one more chance.

I arrived here at the recovery center on a Friday, ███. I had a half open mind when I got here because I knew I needed help. What I found here blew my mind. People are actually happy and not on drugs and alcohol. This, I've never seen. I wanna be one of these people, I wanna be happy. I wanna live my life for the Lord Jesus Christ.

* Department of Corrections

This is where I are at with my life right now. If there is any-thing you can do or say to help me be happy I would greatly appreciate it.

Sincerely,

Heaven's sweet

Hell's hot

you're going to one

ready or not!

Where is Your God Now?

I have been doing drugs for awhile now. My name is Sherry and I'm Desperetely looking for peace. Something I have not had in my Life for a-while. I'm only going back about a year. But you can go back so much futher & see Gods hand in every thing. Let me Start by letting you know a little about my family. My father is a pastor. My Step mom is a minister also. My mom is a Christain too. She lives in Shreveport La. That is also were I'm from. →

I am an addict. My drug! that really has gotten is ~~crack~~ Crack. I have been addicted to crack since 18 yrs old. I'm 31 yrs old now. I have been addicted to drug since 16 yrs old. About a year ago well over a year ago I meet ~~more~~ this man. He was my drug dealer. He came in my life and I thought he was one of the best things that ever happened to me. The reson why is because he told me that if I wanted to be w/ him that I had to stop using crack. So I did. So In my head I thought that he was wonderful. I started helping him sale it to my so called friends. I also didnt tell you that I have a son ● yrs old & a little girl ● yrs old not by him but some one else

The ~~one~~ have been staying w/ my Dad & Stepmom. You see God delivered my of addiction ~~[redacted]~~. But I allowed the devil to steal that back. By covering my sin instead of bring it to the light. I messed up & didn't want to tell anybody because I didn't want to let them down. So I started to smoke crack until I meet this guy. Well it worked for a few month a than I started smoking & ~~[redacted]~~ not letting him know. The first time I slipped & told him. He said I need to get help. So I wont to Dallas TX. to stay w/ friend. a week later I flew him up there. Dallas was not the answer I started →

using ICE. Its like meth
He did not seem to care
if I used that. You see
he snorted cocain and to
him that was okay. So
together we snorted ICE &
Cocain. I realy belived this
was better because I was
not smoking it. Boy the
lies we believe. Both of us
got a job w/ the people we
were staying with. These
people wore my friends not
his. We got into it with
my friends and left. We
went back to Gulfport ms.
He started to sale drugs
again. I tried to look for
a job when we got back
but we were living place
to place. Some time in
Jan. ██████ he let me
hold some crack for him
about two hundred dollars
worth. He did not come

back for 2 days. I smoked
the crack. most all of it
there was about $80 left
He came home and wanted
it. See what I didn't
know then is that he was
smoking too. So the crack
that he was supose to
sale was gone & he came
back for the rest and I
had smoked it. That was
the first night he beat
me. He beat me so bad
I could not even open my
eyes for 3 days. I remember
making peace w/ the Lord
that night. He stuck a
gun down my mouth &
pulled the triger. You see
I didn't know that there
was no bulets in the
gun. After he did that

he took the butt of the
gun and hit me about
for 9 times in the head.
He had all ready been hitting
me kicking me slaming
my head into a brick
wall. I never forget him
saying to me were I your
God know. All I could do is
say Jesus. He looked at
me and told me that he
was Satan. After beating
me for 2 hours he told
me that I was going to
get his money back. So he
gave me some pain killer
told me he was sorry. All
I could do is beg him not
to leave me. Boy I was
sick. He took me to the
mans house the man gave
him $200 to sleep w/ me
He said I could smoke some
crack so I wouldn't hurt.
The same thing he just beat
me for I could now do w/.

I'll never forget I was so
scared we went to the
mans house. He gave them
the money. I want to the
back room. The man felt
sorry for me so we started
talking. All of a sudden
the guy I was seeing came
into the room and said
come on. You see he never
~~noted~~ intended for me to
sleep w/ the man. So I got
up & left. Well that was
the ~~begin~~ start of the beating
and boy did they come. The
month of April I had black
eyes for ~~one month~~ the whole
month. I also found out
that he was smoking crack
& ~~so~~ cheating on me w/
~~so~~ everyone. ~~B~~ But I still
Loved him. I knew some →

thing had to happen. Because he was going to "kill me" quiker than the crack. My family & kids had to stand by & watch this. ~~The~~ I tried to stay a way the best I could. But they are my family and the knew. what was going on. My life just got out of control. The more he ~~did~~ hit me the more I started to hurt me self by cutting ~~on my~~ my arm. This is what they called Self mutilation. I started to smoke crack more. Well this went on. ~~Other~~ I also had Some drug charges before I meet him. I was having to deal w/ thoughs to. My life was really getting out of controll at this point. It was ██████████. The guy I was with was all ways & leaving me at the place we were staying. I was hungry

tired and ~~too~~ didn't know when
he was coming back. He left
me all the time at this point.
Driving my ~~car~~ car & wouldn't
leave the food stamp card
so I could eat. This one night
~~████████████████████~~. He left me
the car ~~because~~ I was
~~████████~~ getting pretty up set.
I drove around trying to
find some crack. ~~████~~ had al
ready beat me up. I was up
set & driving. ~~████~~ This guy
came up to me & I asked
~~████████~~ If he had some
money for gas. He said
follow him he had some
at his house. Any way
he ~~wrote~~ raped me. He had
a knife to my ~~██~~ neck &
raped me. On April ~~██~~04
~~████████████~~ my 31st B-Day.
a week later ~~████████████~~ →

340

the guy I was with told
me I had to check into
the metal hospital so I
did there is were I told
them about the rape. They
talked me into telling
the guy I was with. A month
later I watched ████ the guy
I was with cut this mans
leg almost off. ⌇⌇⌇⌇⌇⌇
I had to watch.. I told him
I forgive him please thats
enough. He let him go.
Needless to say the man in
jail for 7 counts of rape.
Thats not including mine.
from there things got worries
He keep staying a way then
He would come back This
keep going on for a while..
████ until one day I
had the car he pulled up
and said "Go get your life
together and I call you." He
was in the car with two
girls. Always telling me he was

Cheating. well I didn't really
no ▓▓ what to do or where
to go. my parent were not
home. my grandmother had
died and the were going ▓▓
out of town to help w/ that.
So I drive down the street
& See this guy that was
▓▓▓▓ enemy. His name was
▓▓▓ he sold drugs but did
not do them. I told him that
me & ▓▓▓ were having
problems. I also told him that
I need to make some money.
See he was ▓▓▓▓ known
to pimp out girls. He gave
me something to smoke and
said come back in an hour.
So I did. What I didn't know
at that time ▓▓▓ sleep with
▓▓▓▓▓ his girlfriend.
So at the time he was trying
to get him back. We ended

up ▓▓ together. He fell for
me hard. Well ▓▓. found
out got mad came
looking for me w/a
gun shot at us. ▓▓▓▓
I went to police & I ended
up in jail ▓▓▓▓ for old
fines. They are still looking
for ▓▓▓ for that. Went
back to ▓▓▓ Got raped
again by another man.
▓▓▓▓▓▓▓▓ Some were
in between that. Also had
to go to court for possession
charge ▓▓▓▓▓▓▓▓▓▓
Anyway. I plead guilty
got 3yrs probation. Thing
▓▓▓▓ got worries.
Started smoking crack
with him now. He never
let me out of his sight.
Violated my probation &
was running from mdoc.
I also jumped bond on
▓▓▓▓ another charge

mis. Charge. Anyway he took me to my parent house. I was going to turn my self ~~in~~ in to ~~most~~ MDOC. But while I was at my parents house I started to ~~~~ think that this man was going to kill me quicker than crack. I was telling people that I was willing to die that how much I loved ~~~~ him. But PRAISE God that he had his hand on me the ~~~~ whole time. I prayed at my parent house to please remove this feeling from me. I knew at that time that only God could help me. He did. He took those feelings from me. I still didn't turn my self in.

But he did something.
~~to do to go~~ I left with that
guy ███. And I keep
smoking but God still
moved in my Life. I woke
~~up up~~ up one morning in a
motle 6. I was ~~liv~~ living
~~not~~ motle to motle. But these
afternoon when I woke up
God told me I was going
to Jail. Thirty min. later I
was in Jail. I was ~~████~~ so
happy to go to Jail. Tired
of running from ████████
the police. While I was in
Jail my probation officer
told me I was going to
A&D in Rankin (prison)
He told me this was going
to happen. Well God said
diffrent. Some one gave me
an applacation to a Christian
Mission. I filled it out. But
diant think much of it.
Well ████████████ I went to

Court ~~my self~~ my probation
officer didn't show up. Well
God sent me to a rehab center
He is know moving in my
life. It so wonderful. I'm
going to keep pressing in.
I ~~know~~ know his going to help
my addiction he has. I give
him the glory for everything
I prasie him for everything
He is turning my bad into
good right now. Well Thank
you for ~~letting you~~ letting
me tell you.   Love

RH's Note:
Satan sure can make
a mess of your life!

Save for the grace of
God the story you just
read could be yours.

Won't Somebody Help Me?

Dear Hellfighters,

I read your storyies about how Jesus save yall. I was amaze by them. Well here my stories. I've grew up in the street life drugs and thugs all I knew. I was 14teen year old when my downfalls really kick in. Though I've been a sinner before then.

I've never exspect to be in prison reading all these ~~store~~ stories about sins. All these years I was feeling on top of the world and lost it all. I've been in and out of jail so much I've become costom to the life.

When I ~~just~~ try to turn to God it was harder then I thought I backslided every time. Well I'm now 22 years old and securing 5 years 6 month in Tomoka CI for my sins I done. My chaple gave me this hellfighters bible and it touch my soul for yall all inspire me in so many ways. I wish I could've of read it soon then now. I have 4 years left to do but I'm afaid of what happen when my times done.

I've got an mother that preys for me and a loving family. I don't have spiritual mentors here or there. Please help me though this prey for me for I'm a rotten sinner tryings to change his life. I was bampatize Jan 6th ▓▓▓▓

Need spiritual friends out there and here I really whish to change. I've been though to many homes and lost to many friends. This letter is a call for help.

This Hellfighters "handbook" search and rescue open my eyes. I don't exspect yall to corraspond to this letter for I'm a I mate for some bads things but I need help and my mom said God Forgives us for our mistakes we me. well I thank you for taken the time to read this romdom letter from a unknowen inmate but my heart told me to write this to yall.

My name is ~~[redacted]~~ ~~[redacted]~~.

P. S. please Help me Grow with God.

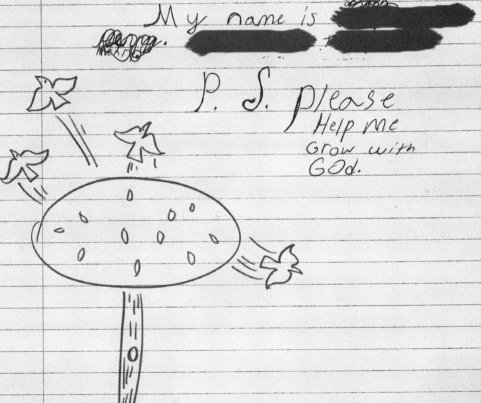

Wow! I'm Living Proof That Jesus Works

I look back on my Life How it was then And how it is now after Almost 14 months being here And how God has blessed me in every way. Since I truly started trusting him. I can remember before I got to the mission how I was nothing but a miserable mess. And now I have dreams and faith. I really understand what it means to have peace, true peace without worrying about ~~world~~ Worldly things I face ~~the~~ life now with prayer and I see things before my eyes that I would ~~ever~~ never believed has happen to a drunk like me; but I began craving the bible like I use to Crave Whiskey And now my life really means something. And I am so blessed to face my past with Jesus in my heart like my fines, childsupport family matters and Just living life on lifes terms I finally realized that Patenience is worth the wait. I never knew ~~a~~ God like I do now I te like problems don't get to me like they use to. I have a true way of facing them now. I'm about to start my life with a lady that the Lord Sent to me and in my heart I really have no dorts or fears cause every time we read the Word together We are Closer than ever.

OVER ⟶

And when we have prayed together in the Past God worked it out Just like his word says. I have never had a relationship ever like this one. I asked the lord over a year ago to lead and Guide my life and if it be his will to Send me a soul mate one day and he did. I remember telling her that I had nothing to offer her I'm in Rehab, broke, but I had the Lord and she said thats why she wanted me and I know it was meant to be. I know I laugh to much but I choose to look at the good out oF All BAD, to know it could Be worse. I choose to be happy, through BAD times, and not dwell on Negativity, And woRRyment. CAuse the lord sAys thats oF the devil. My LiFe At this moment is with Jesus in my heaRt, Bible in my hand, and A Future with my wiFe And the HellFighteRs Christian Ministry FRom m/c shop to giving out tRacks, And PRaising Jesus EveRyday CAuse His woRd is the truth I'm Living Proof. Amen!

THE REALITY

Nearly everyone who comes to a Mission at the Cross facility, or any one of the thousands of other recovery centers across the country, wants to walk out with the promise that their dream of a better way of life will be fulfilled. However, no recovery center can promise that, but Jesus can, and will. Yes, He will fulfill His promise to make all things right, if... the person who truly wants his dream to be fulfilled will do whatever it takes to make it happen.

Nearly every testimony you have read in this book ends with, I love Jesus; I've found the perfect peace; I love my Bible and I read it every day; I pray, I praise, I worship! My old life is gone; I now have a new beginning, etc. Everyone who says these things **means them**, until they step back into the real world. Then, except for a few, the rest of their story picks up right where it left off when they entered a recovery center.

I'm not being negative-just honest!

A lasting relationship with Jesus is the key to any recovering addict's success, but...encouragement from family and friends also helps bring the recovery process to fruition. An addict cannot become the person they dream of becoming overnight. It takes a while. That's why many facilities like Mission at the Cross offer extended stay options. Experience has proven that thirty, sixty and ninety day programs lay the groundwork for recovery, but six, twelve and twenty-four month programs, even though not guaranteed, bring about phenomenal success for those who want their life back. It's a fact that Jesus can save the vilest wretch on earth, but it still takes time, for them to fall deeply in love with Jesus.

Pen and ink cannot explain the grip and monstrous effect that drugs and alcohol have on a person. Unless you've experienced addiction personally, or have been close enough to these monsters to feel the pain, smell the stench, take the punches, hear the growls, combat the anger, wipe up the vomit, mop up the pee or give a cup of coffee to a guy who has lost everything, then you really don't have a clue. The monsters of addiction are literally a foretaste of hell.

If you, a loved one, or someone you know, is caught up in this web of horror, then let's do something about it together. Contact a Jesus-based recovery center in your area and get yourself, or whoever is struggling, there as fast as you can.

If your heart's been touched by the content of this book and the desperation revealed in these letters and you want to do something about it, become involved with a Jesus-based recovery center in your area. You'll never know what a difference you could make in a life.

(If you don't know of a Jesus-based recovery center in your area, contact us at missionatthecross.com and we'll do our best to help you find one.)

My Name is Crystal Meth

I'll destroy your home
and tear your family apart.
I'll steal your children,
and that's just the start.

I'm more valued than diamonds,
more precious than gold.
The sorrow I bring,
is a sight to behold.

If you need me, remember,
I'm easily found.
I live all around you,
in schools and in town.

I live with the rich,
I live with the poor.
I live down the street,
maybe next door.

I'm made in a lab,
but not one like you think.
I'm sometimes made
under your sink.

I'm made in your closets,
and in the woods.
If this scares you to death
it certainly should.

I have many names,
but there's one you know best.
I'm sure you've heard of me
my name's Crystal Meth.

My power is awesome,
just try me and see.
But if you do,
you may never break free.

Try me just once,
and I might let you go.
But try me twice,
and I'll own your soul.

When I posses you,
you'll steal and you'll lie.
You'll do whatever
it takes to get high.

The crimes you'll commit
for my narcotic charms,
will be worth the pleasure
you'll feel in my arms.

You'll lie to your mother.
and steal from your dad.
When you see their tears,
you'll never feel sad.

You'll forget your morals
and how you were raised.
Then I'll be your conscience,
and teach you my ways.

I take kids from their parents,
and parents from their kids.
I turn people from God,
and I separate friends.

I'll take everything from you,
your looks and your pride.
I'll be with you always,
right by your side.

You'll give up everything,
family and home,
your money and friends,
then you'll be alone.

I'll take and take,
till you've no more to give.
Including your purpose
and will to live.

If you try me be warned,
this is not a game.
If given the chance,
I'll drive you insane.

I'll ravage your body,
and control your mind.
I'll own you completely,
your soul will be mine.

I'll give you a nightmare
when you're in your bed.
And voices you'll hear,
from inside your head.

The sweats and shakes,
and the visions you'll see.
I want you to know
they're all gifts from me.

But then it's too late,
and you'll know in your heart,
that you are now mine,
and we shall never part.

You'll regret that you tried me
(they always do).
But you came to me,
not me to you.

You never thought this would happen,
even though you were told.
But you challenged my powers,
and chose to be bold.

You should have said no,
and then walked away.
If you could live that day over,
now what would you say?

My powers are awesome,
as I told you before.
I'll take your life
and make it hunger for more.

I'll be your master,
and you'll be my slave.
And then I'll take you
straight to your grave.

Now that you've met me,
what will you do?
Will you give me a try?
It's all up to you.

I can show you more misery
than words can tell.
Come, take my hand,
and I'll lead you to Hell!!!

So now that you know me,
what will YOU do?
Take MY advice
and DON'T BE A FOOL!

RH's Note:
There is a way that
seemeth right unto a
man [or woman], but the
end thereof is the way of
death (Proverbs 16:25,
paraphrased).

"A League of Extraordinary
Ladies & Gentlemen
Who Are On Fire For Jesus!"

Richard has written many books, including:

A Redneck's Guide to Financial Freedom
A Soulwinning Guide for Hellfighters
America's Churches Through the Eyes of a Bum
Book of John - Paraphrased
Love Letters from a King
One Moment in Time
Poor Richard's Proverbs
The Circular Rings of Kansas
The Enemy of Heaven
The Final Destination
The Final Play
The Hellfighter Trilogy:
The Call
The Commission
The Conflict
The Magical Mulberry Tree
The Seven Churches
The Treasures of Solomon
The Well
Why Everybody Needs Jesus
You Can Do It

Richard has also written Gospel tracts, including:

EGBAR

Guardian Angels

Halloween—What's It Really All About?

Have a Great Day!

Have a Great Tomorrow

Have a Safe Journey

Hellfighters

I'm Here for the Party

In the Company of Fish

Is Hell Right for You?

Jesus Loves You

Journey to Abundant Life

Keeping Christ in Christmas

Merry Christmas

Nickel Tissue

Orange Vestitis

Richard the Rhino Man

Running On Empty

SATAN SUCKS

Something Special

The Amazing Ride

The Black Plane

The Happy Ending

The Treasure

The Ultimate Fix

The Ultimate Ride

The War Wagon

The World is Ablaze

There's Only One Thing Better Than a Hummer

What's On Your Mind?

Will Someone Plant a Tree for You?

You're Invited to a Bar-B-Q

Some books and tracts are out of print, but may still be available through various sources. Go to www.hellfighters.org or send an e-mail to info@hellfighters.org to order books and other items that are available. If we've got it in stock, then you've got it. If we don't have it, we'll tell you who may have it and where you might be able to get it. If nobody has 'em, it means you've waited too late and missed out.

It's OK to miss out on these books, but don't mess around and miss out on Heaven.

Other Hellfighter Productions
Keeping Christ in Christmas – audio CD
Christians Still Die – 15-minute documentary
The Hellfighter Experience – documentary
The Mission – documentary
Hellfighters/Sturgis – documentary
Last Ounce of Courage – feature film

HEAVEN'S SWEET,
HELL'S HOT,
YOU'RE GOING TO ONE,
READY OR NOT!

Hellfighter Publications
One Freedom Square, Laurel, MS 39440-3367
601-649-1977
www.hellfighters.org • info@hellfighters.org

368